FORGED
through
FIRE

FORGED
through
FIRE

A Reconstructive
Surgeon's Story of Survival,
Faith, and Healing

Mark D. McDonough, MD

Revell

a division of Baker Publishing Group
Grand Rapids, Michigan

© 2019 by Mark D. McDonough

Published by Revell
a division of Baker Publishing Group
PO Box 6287, Grand Rapids, MI 49516-6287
www.revellbooks.com

Printed in the United States of America

Library of Congress Cataloging-in-Publication Data is on file at the Library of Congress, Washington, DC.

ISBN 978-0-8007-3654-5 (pbk.)

Some names and details have been changed to protect the privacy of the individuals involved.

Published in association with the literary agency of Legacy, LLC, 501 N. Orlando Ave., Suite 313–348, Winter Park, FL 32789.

19 20 21 22 23 24 25   7 6 5 4 3 2 1

This book is dedicated to the loving memory and lives of my birth family, including my parents, Dorothy Ann McDonough and Thornton David McDonough, and my brothers Toby (Thomas) Christopher McDonough, Patrick Hardman McDonough, and Timothy Joseph McDonough, along with my surviving brother, Daniel Thornton McDonough.

It is further dedicated with love to my present family, including my wife, Joan Galbraith McDonough, and my sons, Connor, Riley, and Toby.

Contents

Contents

1
AUGUST 3, 1976

I woke perspiring as an intense wall of heat rolled across the room. A glance at the clock revealed less than an hour since I had turned in for the night. Loud cracking noises pulled me from sleep. In the orange glow, my eyes started to water and burn like they'd been too long in an over-chlorinated pool, yet I had not been swimming.

I sat up groggily as thoughts skittered through my sleep-hazed mind: *I'm in my own bed. Dad is out of town: San Francisco.*

"You're the man of the house now, chum," he had told me before leaving. "Use your head and help your mom with your brothers."

Then, like a searchlight blasting through the fog, came the awful realization: *The house is on fire! I have to get everyone out!*

Jumping out of bed I noticed a rolling, dense smoke as it cast a thick blanket up from the first floor and into the second story of our colonial home. It was compact, nearly impervious to light except for the scarlet hue and intermittent flash of spiking flames darting up through the stairwell like a serpent's tongue striking randomly. I was rooted in place by the unbearable heat; the slightest movement only intensified the pain. I was trapped with nowhere to run. If I had pictured hell in my mind, this would have been it. A burning wall of immense heat was literally degloving my skin.

My breaths were shallow and rapid, each one searing my throat like shards of glass, tearing its lining. The sensation was heightened by the vibrations from my screams of terror and warning.

Tim, first on the evacuation list as he and I shared the room, was close at hand. He heard me before anyone else and was knocking the screen from his window. At fourteen, he was eighteen months younger than I and slept across from me. Our room overlooked the front and side of the house on North Park Drive in peaceful Fairview Park, a suburb on the west side of Cleveland, Ohio.

"Fire!" I shouted as loudly as I could. "Fire! Everybody, get out!"

For another moment I was immobilized. The heat intensified, stinging my skin as I stood in just a pair of swimming trunks. As an enthusiastic competitive swimmer, this was standard wear in the summer so I could be ready to strip down and dive into a pool at a moment's notice. I'd been too lazy to change before hitting the sack.

I am trapped, I thought. *Must find my way out!* But I had to help the others. *Get the family out!*

Somewhere in my periphery, I sensed Tim moving fast nearby, climbing through the window over his bed and dropping down onto the side yard some fifteen feet below.

Shouting "Fire! Fire!" as loudly as I could, though my cries felt strangled, I bolted from our room through the open door, out onto the main landing. Screaming again, I was aware of my younger brothers Danny and Packy scrambling in the room they shared next to ours, each one at different bedroom windows facing the back and side of the house. Like Tim, they pushed their way out through their windows. Danny landed on the garage roof first; Packy chose a fall from the higher side window.

Becoming more and more aware that flames were engulfing our home, I knew that I should escape from a window too. But first I had to be sure that Mom and Toby, my six-year-old youngest brother, got out safely. Their rooms were on the other side of the stairwell, which by now was acting as a chimney through which blazing tongues flickered, attaching themselves to the high-pitched ceiling above.

The flames greedily sucked all oxygen from the core of our house, consuming me with terror and trepidation. The sounds were horrifying, like the bellowing of tornadoes. The walls were being stripped of their paper and my body of its skin. My screams continued, strident and strangled by the suffocating smoke as my blood curdled, coagulating on the surface of my extremities.

The flames continued to tower upward, reaching toward their intended victims. I heard sounds, my own howling with moans of agony, the loud cracks of splintering wood like felled trees. Everything was happening quickly though each moment seemed to last forever.

Desperate for air, I punched my right hand through the glass window in the bathroom, thinking I might first suck down some precious oxygen before hopefully climbing out to safety and reaching Mom via the sundeck attached to her room.

My fist left shards of double-paned glass at my feet and blood-tinged grains embedded in my skin, but I didn't notice the pain. My heart sank as I realized that by slamming on the window I had knocked it off its rails. The sash, with its jagged fragments of glass, now sat diagonally askew, hopelessly jammed.

The smoke continued to get thicker, obstructing all vision and burning my eyes, which were smeared with tears from the fumes. There was still a lurid orange-red glow somewhere beyond the soot-gray cloud around me.

There was no way I could get across the stairwell to the other side of the house and the rooms where Mom and Toby slept. My only option, the only hope, was to somehow get up to the balcony from the back of the house. However, the wooden balcony's railing and its bordering turpentine-filled evergreen trees were already fueling the raging fire. Dad and I had planted those pines years before when I was just a sapling myself.

I stumbled down the stairs and leapt to the front door—but closer to the source of the flames. Crashing down onto the marble foyer, I reached for the handle of the door. It was locked but was designed to unlock and turn easily from the inside. I turned it and pulled, but it didn't move despite my adrenaline-surged might. The door would not budge; firefighters would later determine that the intense heat had caused the metal door to expand, effectively sealing me inside. The thick, heavy smoke, compounded with the burning inferno and oxygen deprivation, was smothering any kind of rational thinking. Somehow, I had the presence of mind to know that wasting more precious seconds trying to open the door was suicidal.

I ran past the family room, the place where we later learned the fire had originated. The burning was at peak intensity, seemingly bent on destroying the very thing for which the room was named, but I thought perhaps I could reach the rear door into the garage.

Ducking my head and partially crouching, I held my hands up in front of my face to protect it from the heat blast. I was aware of fluids oozing all over my skin as it started to blister and peel. Shouting in fury, I hurried through the kitchen, passing alongside the countertop on which sat a half dozen smoke detectors.

Ironically, Dad had tried to install them the night before he left for San Francisco but had been forced to abandon the project when he realized we didn't have the batteries they required. Chased by the far-reaching tendrils of fire, I continued toward the door to the garage—and safety—just a few feet away.

"Dear God," I gasped as I reached for the garage door handle, "please, let me go, lead me out." Then there was blackness. I lost consciousness, my body falling to the floor and blocking the door to the garage. A tenacious firefighter would later recount how he'd had a premonition that a human body was blocking the entry through which he ultimately carried my limp form.

For the second time in an hour I came to, only this time there was no gradual dawning awareness. Instantly I was consumed by unimaginable pain. Every square inch of my body was on fire, my nerves screaming with unbearable intensity.

I repeated the prayer for help I had gasped before passing out. But this time I prayed for God to scoop me into his hands. All I wanted was for him to take me now, immediately. Exactly what had happened was unclear: I knew that some kind of dreadful accident had occurred, that death was somehow near though regrettably not certain. As every nerve ending screamed, the thought of remaining alive for another minute was overwhelming. I just wanted to stop hurting.

I wondered if I might be dead and had somehow arrived at the lake of fire. Just the thought of that possibility caused such an adrenaline surge that I could feel the pounding of my heart in my chest. Then the crackle of a radio cut through my swirling thoughts as another interminable second passed.

Instructions came over a radio and I realized I was lying in an ambulance. "If he's badly burned, go straight to Metro." The dispatcher was sending us to Cleveland Metropolitan General Hospital, with its regional burn unit.

The horror of being trapped in the burning house returned immediately, causing me to shiver as we raced through the streets. We first stopped at Fairview General Hospital—where I had been born—for bottles of saline solution. A paramedic I could vaguely see in my left periphery poured the fluids copiously over my body. Now the shivering was unstoppable and I trembled convulsively. *God, please hear me. Please take me!*

The paramedics needed intravenous access to begin replenishing vital bodily fluids. They were desperately trying—but with minimal success—to prevent me from going into potentially fatal shock. The repeated needle stabs were almost negligible compared with the torture that wracked the rest of my body.

As the ambulance swerved in and out of traffic, sirens blaring, I could feel my body listing right and left. I was desperate to know what had happened to the others. *Where are my mother, Tim, Dan, Packy, and Toby? Are they okay? Did they escape unharmed?* But my attempts to speak were to no avail, resulting in muffled grunts, the noxious effects of smoke and combustion.

Thoughts randomly skated through my head. *I let Dad down. What if Mom and Toby were not rescued in time?* It was all too much to bear. I wanted to die, to escape not only the physical pain but also the mental anguish.

Then I heard one of the paramedics.

"He's probably 60 to 70 percent burned. We're headed to Metro."

Every tiny bump sent shock waves through my body, miniature seizures compounding the already unbearable pain. I knew that things were critical; I was somewhere on the edge of life. I didn't think I could survive the race to the hospital, nor did I want to.

God, why is it taking so dreadfully long to die? My throat was scraped raw, like I'd swallowed razor blades.

Seared, scared, desperate to know what had happened to the rest of my family for whom I'd been responsible, all I could do was endure the pain. One intolerable second would pass only to be followed by another. I had no way of knowing how completely life had changed.

2

ROOTS

My family could have been portrayed in a Norman Rock-
well painting. August 3, 1976, changed that.

Our home had rung with the sounds of laughter and play.
With five young boys, our relatives, and friends, there was
never a shortage of visitors or company.

Mom and Dad, a striking couple with warm and affection-
ate personalities, weren't afraid to demonstrate their love for
each other or their sons. There were always plenty of hugs
and kisses to be shared.

Their journey began when they met at Miami University
of Ohio in the mid-fifties, neither of them concerned about
the seven-year age difference. Dorothy Ann Hardman, from
Olmstead Falls, Ohio, was a strikingly gorgeous twenty-year-
old studying biology. Gregarious, something of a social butterfly, her athletic figure stood nearly five feet seven, befitting
a former cheerleader.

Dorothy had smooth, naturally tanned skin; her light brown hair and high cheekbones were matched with penetrating amber eyes. Her warmly charismatic and ready smile revealed perfect teeth. Always dressed fashionably, Dorothy was usually at the center of a circle of friends who appreciated her witty, often dry sense of humor and infectious laugh.

The older of two girls raised in a Protestant home, she found herself seeing almost eye to eye with Thornton David McDonough. Though T, as everyone knew him, stood only an inch or so taller, his personality projected greater stature. The third of four children, and the only boy born into an Irish-Catholic family from Bay Village, Ohio, he arrived at the university's Oxford campus as an older student, having taken a voluntary two-year hiatus from studies to enlist in the United States Air Force where he became a fighter pilot of the famous F-86D jet.

Dorothy and T fell deeply in love, marrying on June 7, 1958. Though she was teaching high school biology when they tied the knot, my arrival the following year put an end to that as she became a stay-at-home mom, in keeping with the ways and values of the times. Within a few years there were three boys, two cars in the garage, and Sam the collie mix.

On October 25, 1959, I arrived, weighing in at eleven pounds seven ounces and twenty-one inches—all lucky numbers, Dad would say. Seventeen months later Mom gave birth to son number two; Timothy Joseph debuted on May 19, 1961. He would grow into my smiling, cleverly cagey, fun-loving, and joyful partner in many adventures. Fourteen months after Tim's arrival another boy came along; Daniel Thornton was delivered on July 27, 1962. He would become observant, intelligent, witty, sometimes quiet, always charming.

I loved anything outdoors and in any season; as I grew, that would include building forts and swimming during the hot summers, playing football in the fall, and sledding or ice-skating through the freezing cold Ohio winters. Later, during my early teen years, one of my buddies up the street had the perfect yard for flooding with water to fashion a large ice rink. We could be found playing hockey from after school until well into the brisk and windy night, with the rink lighted by garage floods.

Our neighborhood was populated with many similar middle-class to upper middle-class families enjoying the prosperity and growth of the sixties' booming economy. Weekends my parents would entertain at home or attend cocktail parties hosted by any of their numerous friends. The music of Frank Sinatra, Dean Martin, and the rest of the Rat Pack filled the air from the TV stereo console. Many nights I would listen from my bedroom as Mom and Dad and their friends sang along to Johnny Mathis, Roger "King of the Road" Miller, and other popular artists.

In the early days Mom loved dressing us three toddlers up in matching outfits, most notably on special occasions like going out to a restaurant for dinner, neighborhood block parties, and the community fair with its Memorial Day parade. We'd decorate our bikes with crepe paper and streamers, then ride down the blocked streets waving to friends and family with pride.

Though she was busy at home caring for three small boys, Mom never lost her gift for teaching; an avid reader, she passed this love on to me. She was in many ways the center of our home, but it was Dad who loomed large. He projected a confidence and knowledge about the world and his way within it that could at times be intimidating to people unfamiliar with his strong personality and dominant character.

Incredibly resourceful, Dad had a strong work ethic that had been instilled at a young age by his father, one he would in turn impart to his sons. Growing up during World War II, he had worked a variety of sales jobs, selling everything from lightbulbs and newspapers to batteries and magazines.

Having earned a business degree from Miami University, Dad became a life insurance salesman, eventually licensed to broker securities and stocks. He ultimately became vice president and partner at Roulston & Company, a prestigious Cleveland firm. In addition, he was avidly involved in many different organizations and philanthropic endeavors.

Dad always taught us that honesty and integrity were of paramount importance and integral attributes to becoming men, and that a man was only as good as his word. He said that if one believed in his product and himself, he could sell anything: as a "make it happen" kind of guy, he wouldn't take no for an answer.

Indeed, that was how we came to build our dream home on North Park Drive.

Patrick Hardman McDonough arrived on July 15, 1966. Nicknamed "Packy," he was quietly pensive but could also be charming like his older brothers, with a winning smile. With his addition to the mix it was time to look for more space for our growing family.

Dad had his eye on a vacant lot not far from where we were living. It was located on the north side, across the street from Bain Park's thirty-some acres of woods, cackling brooks, old stone bridges, and hiking paths. Dad decided that the corner parcel of land on North Park Drive would be a perfect location. Two mature maple trees stood at the front of the plot, with a weeping willow to the rear.

Adding to the land's appeal was the fact that it was also just four houses down from the local junior and senior high schools. With no plans to develop it, the owner was said to be holding out for a future boom in raw land values, despite having received several prior offers. The ungroomed parcel had long remained no more than a favorite dumping ground for the neighborhood canine population.

One Saturday afternoon, while mowing the front lawn of our three-bedroom ranch, Dad was walloped with sudden inspiration. He halted the mower midway across the yard, killed the engine, and marched resolutely into the house, leaving the mower where it stood. He showered, donned some khaki slacks and a sport shirt, slipped on loafers, and headed out to the car.

Arriving at the lot owner's home, Dad knocked on the front door and was invited inside. There he launched into the heartwarming tale of a young couple's love, and their honest and noble struggle to raise and provide for their Christian family with four boys. Dad told how this humble family might be blessed with the good fortune to build their dream home on a little parcel of heaven in the heart of their beloved community. Their four sons could ride their sleds down the hills of Bain Park each winter. In the summers they could hike and explore its creeks. Elaborating, he described how the boys could also easily walk the short distance to school, and on cool Friday evenings in the fall, their mom and dad could stroll down the street to see the high school football games.

Dad implored the landowner to help an enterprising father realize such a dream for his family—and his sales pitch was successful. A cordial handshake sealed the deal that afternoon.

My father designed the four-bedroom, two-story colonial down to the last inch. It would boast a wood-paneled family room with a brick fireplace and hearth. Adjacent to the fireplace was a built-in woodbox with decorative cabinet doors. The compartment also had an exterior door through which hand-split pine and oak could be loaded from the log pile in our well-maintained side yard. A row of pine trees was planted by Dad, my brothers, and me that grew tall, bordering the east side of the house and yard.

Moving day was memorable. As the movers unloaded furniture and boxes, Timmy, Danny, and I set out to explore the park across the street while Packy watched Mom and Dad from his playpen as they unpacked and decorated our new home.

Bain Park became our playground. We spent many days in our own paradise during all four seasons, hiking, climbing, riding bikes, or sledding down hills with characteristic names like "Jack Rabbit" and "Caterpillar."

Whenever Dad arrived home from the office, we boys would charge to his open arms where one, two, or all three would be lifted into a bear hug. He was always on the lookout for a teaching moment. He'd conduct spontaneous talks on various subjects—always attentive to proper grammar, being the son of an English teacher.

From as young as I can remember, I had always wanted to sleep or camp outdoors. One summer day Dad came home from the office with a pup tent. He changed from his conservative suit and tie, wing tip shoes, and button-down oxford shirt into his khaki pants and sweatshirt.

Then we all went out to the yard to set up the tent. It was basic, just a piece of plastic, four feet by eight feet, that draped over a low clothesline. But at ages five, four, and three, my brothers and I were ecstatic. Dad said we could sleep in the tent overnight, and he would stay with us, too, so that we wouldn't be afraid. He used the whole experience to teach us about the beauty of nature even in the quiet, moon-shadowed darkness.

Another time, while we were still quite young, he wanted to find a way to convince us that we could always trust him and that there was nothing to fear in God's world; God would always be with us. He took us into the basement, explaining that sometimes our greatest fears were imagined.

"Do what you fear and the fear will disappear," he told us. That became one of several family mantras I repeated years later while raising boys of my own.

Taking us behind the furnace, Dad had us all squat down in a small space between an air duct and the wall. No matter what, he assured us, we were safe. Then he turned out the lights while restating gently that no ill fate would befall us. In the dark-as-pitch room, he pounded loudly on the furnace while we laughed nervously, trying to sound brave.

From that day on, I never feared the dark. But even more importantly, I always had a certainty that I could trust my dad, and my heavenly Father, even if the whole world seemed against me.

Dad had a far-reaching wolf whistle produced using only his index finger, thumb, and tongue. Upon hearing it, all sons were to immediately report at attention, front and center. Along with military stance, we knew how to march in single file formation. In time, he developed separate whistles with unique tone changes designated for each of us so that we could be summoned from anywhere in the neighborhood—one son, two sons, three sons, or all four (and later five).

We were also instructed in proper and formal etiquette regarding social introductions to other adults in our parents' circles. Dad emphasized the importance of standing to attention, offering a firm handshake, and looking the new acquaintance squarely in the eye while clearly enunciating, "How do you do, Mr. or Mrs. So-and-So?"

Though Mom and Dad expected good behavior from us, there was never any doubt that my brothers and I were well fed with love. Our parents loved us unconditionally, demonstrating it both verbally and physically. They encouraged us without reservation in all of our endeavors, large or small. And they were always forgiving when we made mistakes or didn't get our manners quite right, teaching us to take responsibility for our own behavior instead of worrying about that of another.

For example, one spring when we were en route to a family vacation in Florida, we stayed at a Holiday Inn. That evening we were getting ready to go to the dining room. All dressed in matching swimsuits, swim jackets, and flip-flops, we marched single file into the restaurant. Mom and Dad beamed with pride that their gentleman sons were so quiet, considerate, and attentive to the others around them.

We could feel the eyes of all the other patrons fixed upon our model family, stately and gallant, with no fighting or squabbling among any of us. Even the potentially stressful choosing from the menus and ordering our food passed without incident.

As the meals were delivered to the table, each child patiently awaited his plate. We politely placed our napkins on our laps and gave thanks to the Lord for our delightful bounty. Suddenly the little blond one, Danny, dropped a chicken leg to the carpet below, prompting him to give a loud shout.

"Oh crud! Now what?"

Mom and Dad blushed the deep red of a fire engine as everyone in the restaurant laughed hysterically. Then, after a second of silence, they too guffawed and laughed as hard as I'd ever seen them.

Family vacations remain the source of some of my fondest memories. Dad taught us each to swim at a very early age, and our summer road trips were to places with water for swimming, boating, skiing, and fishing.

Each October, along with three or four other families, we'd venture to the mountains of Pennsylvania. Early on, the fathers and sons camped in tents. Later, the moms and sisters joined us, and we stayed in Depression-era log cabins along the Clarion River in Cook Forest. We would hike through the woods when the leaves blazed red and crisp yellow. We built log forts deep among the pines and hemlocks, turning them into jails for nighttime games of capture the flag.

In all our adventures, both Mom and Dad instilled in us a passion for nature. Dad was always ready to instruct us on some topic: the stars and constellations, trees, building fires, dead-reckoning navigation, boating and nautical safety, or surviving off the land.

From our first pup tent experience, I gradually cultivated a keen appreciation for anything and everything outdoors. My brothers and I were all Boy Scouts and were especially active in many camping excursions and adventures, including the well-known Winter Klondike and the French River canoe trips in Canada. I also enjoyed backpacking.

Out in the wild I learned survival skills and acquired the attitude needed to exercise them effectively—little knowing that later in life I would need to do so in a completely different survival mode, concentrating all of my efforts to stay alive.

3

RESCUE

I had no idea what time it was when I was bundled into the ambulance. Seemingly every fiber in my body screamed for relief from the pain as our home on North Park Drive burned. But the emergency team had a close eye on the clock: they were in a race against time.

The first hour following a major trauma is the critical time during which every decision and intervention may be the difference between life and death—to first responders it is known as the "golden hour." In my case it meant sixty minutes for them to save my life before the massive trauma simply swallowed me.

Doctors roughly calculate the mortality or likelihood of burn death by adding the age of the victim to the percentage of burns relative to their total body surface area. Sixteen years of age plus burns to 60 to 70 percent of my nearly naked body indicated that I had roughly a 20 percent chance or less of surviving.

All I knew was that I was engulfed in a fireball of terrible pain. Making matters worse, I could hardly breathe and barely see. Equally concerning, I was dying of thirst, desperate for water. I coughed and hacked, straining to suck air into my smoke-filled lungs, but doing so only seemed to further sear my already raw throat lining.

Any attempt at speech was excruciating; my throat was so parched I could barely make sounds, and my airway was already swelling toward closure. I was desperate to know what had happened: were Toby and Mom okay? But it was hard to do more than croak, and then even those attempts to communicate were thwarted as one of the ambulance crew pressed an oxygen mask against my face.

Adding to my already heightened state of anxiety, I could not see clearly enough to know what was going on around me. My eyes were stinging, irritated by smoke, my vision blurred by more than fearful tears. I tried to blink but my focus was still hazy, like trying to see through a screen of cheesecloth. My hearing was muffled too, with mostly unintelligible chatter and sounds in my periphery. Intermittently, I'd pick up a snatch of what was being said, such as the radio exchange redirecting us to Metro.

It was hard to make sense of everything that was happening. I seemed to be caught in a kaleidoscope of shifting shadows, sounds, and sensations. What was all too clear, though, was the pain. I was desperate for some kind of relief for my desiccated throat but none came. *Water. Please give me some water!* All I could do was try to float on each roll of pain as it crashed over me like waves breaking on jagged rocks of a storm-beaten beach—unremitting, relentless.

It was as though I'd been skinned alive with a sharp steel blade and then bathed in alcohol. Every square inch of my body's surface appeared to be burning, incinerating. Millions of exposed nerve endings in my arms, back, stomach, and legs shrieked together. It felt like hot, molten pillows were smothering my face. Even my urine was inflamed as it spilled hot from my body. I just wanted to die, but the perpetual burning reminded me that I was regretfully still alive.

I felt hands on me, pushing my body this way and that as the vehicle hummed along. Though I was unable to voice it aloud, inside I screamed, *Dear God! Please take me now! I can't take one more second of this pain! Oh my God, please!*

While my body continued its cremation, it was simultaneously trying to manage the massive trauma it had sustained, causing me to shiver violently. Slipping into a state of shock, my body was doing whatever it could in an all-out effort to survive, while in my head I wanted the relief that could only come from death.

My skin was multitasking and performing each of its physiological functions at their peak levels of intensity. It was desperately attempting to regulate temperature along with fluid shifts across its surface between my dynamically changing blood vessels and surrounding tissues. It was struggling to fulfill its role as the largest organ in the body. Despite such a lofty title, it couldn't prevent critically devastating edema or the concurrent constriction of my blood vessels; the result was a decline in oxygen delivery to my extremities, tissues, and other vital organs. The potential for total organ failure makes burns the most severe form of trauma.

One of the most important interventions following a large burn injury is replenishing massive amounts of critically vital fluids. The paramedics caring for me eventually inserted a large-bore intravenous (IV) line through which they could replace diminishing fluids and prevent the onset of hypovolemic (low fluid) shock, which could have meant cardiac arrest and even death. Meanwhile, they continued to pour saline solution over me, cooling the burns. The shivering and trembling would not stop as I begged God to take me.

The cardiovascular system is also a major player in response to trauma but can work at an elevated rate for only so long. In injuries where there is a massive amount of blood loss or hypovolemia—such as in a burn injury—the result is sudden hypotension, or drop in blood pressure. Recognizing that it can't keep working at maximal intensity, the heart reduces its output. Alarmingly, perversely, this decreases blood flow to other parts of the body just when it is needed most.

Even if the heart doesn't stop, there could be gastrointestinal or renal failure. The kidneys are especially at risk. If they don't have a steady flow of fluid washing through them they will shut down, resulting in renal failure and ultimately death from toxic buildup of waste.

Burn trauma creates a sort of perfect storm with its threat to life. Given all that they were dealing with in those important early minutes, it is not surprising that the ambulance crew had little time to spend trying to communicate with me, except for telling me to hang in there and we'd be at the hospital as soon as possible.

But it also spared them the task of telling me what they had learned as we headed to Metro: Toby was dead. Firemen had found his small lifeless body under a blanket at the foot of his bed, where he apparently had hidden in fear before dying from asphyxiation.

Mom was on her way to another hospital in a second ambulance, unconscious and clinging to life, having been found on the floor of her bedroom. Her limp body had formed a silhouette on the gold carpet, now charcoal gray from the scorching smoke damage, like the barren outline of a car in a driveway following a heavy snowfall.

Meanwhile, my agony included feeling that I had somehow let Dad down, that I had failed in my responsibilities as the man of the house. *How can I ever face him again—if I live long enough to?*

When we finally arrived at the hospital, I felt like I was the object of some great game of tug-of-war. Hands grasped at me from all directions. I could hear different voices, urgent and strong. Though I knew they were trying to help me, every touch—and there was no time to be tender—hurt. Imagine the worst sunburn you have ever experienced and having someone rub the affected skin hard with sandpaper. Then multiply that a thousand times. That would not be close to how bad it was.

Not surprisingly, I struggled to break free from the grip of those who were only causing me more pain. Firm hands held me down as I was lifted onto the emergency room bed. My arms and legs were pulled in different directions as I wriggled and attempted to pull away. My efforts at calling for help, to ask what was happening, were cut off as someone held my head still.

Essential to survival was getting more oxygen into my system, and that meant I needed to be intubated. A long breathing tube was being pushed down my throat, but I fought and tried to turn away as doctors struggled to insert it. My combative response and their need to act swiftly meant there was no time for niceties, and inserting the tube only resulted in further scraping of my already shredded mucosal tissue. I could taste the blood trickling down my esophagus.

I gagged, only making it harder for me to breathe. I felt as though I was being forced to swallow a garden hose. The procedure was literally choking off any hope I had of speaking.

Irrationally, my anger only intensified when I felt someone cutting my swimsuit away with a pair of scissors. *How dare these people!* I thought. *I'm burning here! Can't anyone see? Help me, please!* For a second, my vision cleared and I could make out bodies in green hospital scrubs moving around me in a swirl. One of them began inserting a urinary catheter.

Someone else was putting gel on my arms, but I couldn't feel it. My body seemed to recognize only pain. *I can't survive another second,* I thought. But then another would pass, and then another. *Dear God, please take me! I'll do anything to end this.* I snapped my head violently from side to side, trying to force the tube out of my mouth so my breathing would stop. My neck and face were burning, like acid was eating through my skin inch by inch, deeper and deeper. *Oh dear God!*

I was in a state of hyper-anxiety, on the edge of panic. The next assault came as I felt sharp needles entering my arms and both sides of my neck. I caught a snippet of the exchanges that were continuing.

"We're giving you medicine for pain. We need better access! We need better access!"

A hard X-ray plate was forced behind my burning back as I tried to sit up, only to be pushed back down. Cold and sharp, the board seemed to cut into me. Then someone else repositioned the breathing tube, further cutting into the mucosal lining of my throat and bringing more tears to my eyes. Tissue first damaged by heat and smoke inhalation was now scraped raw, and it left me yearning for even a drop of water.

I can't breathe! God, please, please end this now!

But there was worse to come.

As my body continued to swell, it was beginning to sort of squeeze itself to death, like a python coiling around its victim. Beneath the skin and surrounding the body's muscle is a tissue known as fascia, a fibrous substance like the strapping tape used to wrap packages for mailing. When the skin is burned away, this underlying fascia tightens because of the increased swelling. The fascia can then cause compression of the underlying muscles, vessels, and nerves, resulting in necrosis: the affected parts of the body die for lack of adequate blood flow.

In such situations, the pressure must be relieved—and quickly. There is no time for formalities. So ER doctors perform fasciotomies, cutting through the fascia to give the tissues underneath some breathing room, as it were. It is a bit like opening a tube of ready-to-bake cinnamon bun dough; the freed contents swell and expand as they burst out. Opening the skin and fascia in this way decompresses the vital vessels and nerves below, restoring essential blood flow. And so I was hit by another wave of pain as doctors sliced into the flesh of my arms and chest. I could feel the blades cutting into me—a cold shiver deep inside. It was a different kind of pain from the burns.

The agony continued despite reassurances. Someone leaned down close to my ear, saying, "We're giving you something in your IV for the pain." It seemed to go on forever, and I continued to pray that I could somehow just die. But at some point the doctors must have decided I was going to make it. The urgent activity slowed, and I was taken from the ER bay to the intensive care section of the burn unit, ten floors higher. My body and the burns were wrapped in some kind of wet gauze. The following minutes and hours would be touch and go, let alone the days or weeks.

Feeling that I was being ignored as so many people assaulted me had been bad enough, but now it seemed like I had been abandoned as I lay still and alone. I sensed one or two nurses scampering about, coming by to check on me from time to time, but otherwise it was quiet. The swelling in my neck, along with the burning sensation in my face, neck, torso, and extremities, severely restricted my mobility and prevented me from turning my head to follow the winding course of the nurses in and out of my field of vision.

Adding to my sense of isolation was the fact that anyone who came into my room needed to be fully gowned and masked to minimize the chance of infection. All I could see were people's eyes scanning quickly up and down my body.

Restrained and unable to communicate because of the breathing tube, I was flooded with an overwhelming sense of powerlessness and profound fear. *What is going to happen to me? What has happened to Mom? To Toby? What will Dad say?*

At some stage during those first blurry hours at the hospital, I got at least one answer. I don't remember exactly how they did it, but one of the nurses told me that my loving, angelic brother Toby hadn't made it out of the house and that Mom was in critical condition. Grief overwhelmed even the pain as hot tears filled my eyes. I couldn't believe my poor baby brother was gone.

My thoughts turned to Dad: he had lost a son and his wife was at death's door. *How is he receiving the news and how is he doing? Where is he?*

He arrived on my second day in the ICU. Joe Rattigan had awakened him at 4:00 a.m. in his San Francisco hotel room. The Rattigans lived just a few houses up the street from us on North Park Drive. They were close family friends with whom we shared more than love and Irish heritage: my brothers and I called Joe and his wife, Barbara, uncle and aunt. We considered their children our cousins. One of their boys, Paul, was one of my best buddies growing up.

Police called to the fire had taken Tim, Dan, and Packy to the Rattigans' home, and Joe had accepted the unenviable task of calling his dear friend to break the terrible news. He courageously and directly explained, "Toby is with Christ. Dorothy and Mark are in critical condition. Tim, Dan, and Packy are safe with us."

Later, I learned that Dad had paused for several minutes outside my room in the burn ICU, looking through the window before entering. He needed to steady himself, finding it hard to acknowledge that the grotesquely swollen, swathed figure with tubes and hoses coming from all directions was his oldest son.

He did his best to disguise whatever he may have been feeling inside as he came over to me in a surgical gown and mask. I had determined that I was not going to cry. He had so much to deal with already; I didn't want to add to his load by revealing how much physical and emotional agony I was going through.

Speechless, Dad put his hand gently on me as he bent over and kissed my forehead, ignoring the ointment covering one of my few exposed parts. As I looked into his glassy eyes, I could not remember ever having felt such sadness and love for someone else.

No words were needed. I could see the intense vulnerability in his gaze. As he gently held my bandaged hand, tears rolled down our cheeks. The regret I'd been feeling at having let Dad down was easily overwhelmed by the sorrow and anguish I felt for him and by a powerful awareness of his love for me. I longed to just be enveloped in a hug.

When he did speak, Dad offered healing words that soothed some of the burns in my heart.

"It wasn't your fault, son," he told me. "You're a hero! You got your other brothers out of the house."

He paused. "It was just Toby's time," he went on. "God called him home early."

I couldn't begin to imagine the strength he must have had to say those words, let alone get through those early days after the fire. One son was dead. A second was in intensive care, dangerously close to death. His wife was being kept alive by machines in another hospital. Three other boys were emotionally distraught, one also nursing a broken arm: Packy had fractured his left forearm in his two-story jump to safety.

Exhaustion and excruciating pain combined to make the next couple days a blur. A heavy pall enveloped me emotionally, while everything outside was shrouded in what felt like a thick black blanket. In my conscious moments I begged God for a little mercy, a moment of numbness, just some relief from all the hurt.

Perhaps, I thought, my body and mind had reached their physical and emotional limits. But there was more: Dad told me the day after his return that we needed to think about letting the doctors take Mom off life support. He said that her lungs had been too seriously damaged from smoke inhalation.

Somehow the news didn't really sink in; it was as though I had no room for any further pain. But perhaps, I thought, I should find some room, as I was probably going to need it.

4

BROKEN

Whoever says "What you don't know can't hurt you" is horribly wrong. Fear of the unknown can cause a deep wound, and those chaotic early hours following the fire reawakened memories that only heightened the trauma.

While the surface of my body was screaming with pain that was like a searing, bright flame, inside I was tumbling into an old darkness. Memories of being manhandled by medical personnel years earlier flooded my mind—doctors and nurses so focused on trying to keep me alive they had no time to explain to me what was going on. But in the absence of information, every procedure seemed like it was intended only to cause more pain.

Part of the rising panic I experienced in the ambulance and the Metro ER was triggered by remembering another time when I'd been at the mercy of seemingly unfeeling adults. The experience had embedded in me a strong but forgotten sense of hospitals as places of powerlessness and uncertainty, where patients have little if any control.

At the age of five, I had just started kindergarten when I began to experience intermittent pain in my legs. Sharp shocks would skitter suddenly up and down my lower extremities, from my hips to my feet, when I walked. It became progressively more difficult to lift my legs off the couch or out of bed. Even standing from a sitting position was painful and required all of my effort.

Having always been an active kid, I was now finding it a challenge to walk or run. My hands also were getting weaker, my grip strength draining away. I could no longer apply enough pressure to turn the knobs or release the handles of doors. I didn't really know how to explain to Mom and Dad what was going on, so I just told them that I was achy. They were sympathetic to my complaints, but like most parents probably would, they dismissed what was happening as growing pains that would likely pass with time.

One night, I instinctively grabbed for a nearby plunger to help me balance while climbing down from the toilet. Using it as a crutch, I slowly walked out of the bathroom to the living room couch, complaining that my legs hurt too much to play. This got their attention. The next day Mom made an appointment to see Dr. Roche, our pediatrician.

Early the next day we arrived at his office, me walking slowly with the support of my plunger cane. The nurse helped me onto a scale to check my weight and height. The next thing I knew, Dad, who had snuck in behind me, was lifting me off. He had come from his office to meet us as a surprise. I was glad to see him but also concerned: *There*

must be something seriously wrong with me if he's inter-
rupted his day and left work to come to the appointment.

Dr. Roche finally came into the room with my chart in his hand. He was an elderly gentleman with thinning gray hair, narrow bespectacled eyes, and hands wrinkled with age spots. His facial expressions were serious and earnest. He asked a lot of questions as he performed a full physical examination. Other than the questions, he said very little until asking Mom and Dad to follow him to his office.

Minutes later, when Mom and Dad returned, they explained that I needed to be admitted to Lakewood Hospital for some tests. They also said that I'd be there overnight, possibly for several nights. They couldn't stay with me, but they would come during visiting hours. I knew it was time to be brave.

As we drove into the city, my mood seemed to absorb the melancholy of a cloudy Cleveland afternoon. A friendly elderly lady in admissions informed us that there was no dedicated pediatric floor and I'd be assigned to a regular medical ward. I felt old enough to handle it, but later I really wished there were some kids around just to talk with.

After I was admitted, Dad took me for a mini tour of the floor by way of wheelchair. We went down to the waiting room, where there was a large aquarium filled with various species of fish, including neons. I was mesmerized by their iridescent blue and red stripes.

As I watched, I became hypnotized and relaxed as they schooled about the tranquil aquarium. Outings from my room to the waiting room to watch the fish would become a recurring activity when Mom and Dad visited. That along with playing Candy Land helped to pass the time while demanding little physical strength or dexterity.

The lights, the smells, the sounds all around were unfamiliar and scary. After returning to my room, Mom and Dad tried to make me feel settled. All too soon the intercom sounded.

"Visiting hours are now over. Visiting hours are now over. They will resume again tomorrow at 4:00 p.m."

As the nurses came and lifted me from the wheelchair into a large crib with railings, Mom reminded me that I was never truly alone. Jesus would keep and protect me always, she said. She told me about a time in her childhood when she was very sick with a high fever and was praying fervently. She had looked up and suddenly seen angels at the foot of her bed, she said. Dad smiled warmly and then wrapped his arms around me. He said that they'd return tomorrow as early as they could—and they would bring me something special. Try as I might, I couldn't stop a few tears from escaping; I just wanted to hold him tight and not let go.

Mom licked her fingers and used them to gently part my hair from my forehead. She cradled me in her arms and softly kissed me, placing her warm hand on my cheek. Then she slowly rocked me as she supported me in a sitting position. I tried to hug her back, but my arms felt too weak and I could barely lift them from my sides.

The tender moment was interrupted by the arrival of a stern-looking elderly nurse with gray curly hair flattened across the top of her head by a stiff white cap. She had black, beady eyes deeply inset behind glasses framing her wrinkled face. She reminded me of a Mr. Potato Head that had been left to shrivel up for several weeks on a shelf.

"Mom and Dad," she announced coldly, "you're going to have to leave now. Visiting hours were over five minutes ago. You can come back to visit the youngster tomorrow."

I heard Mom say quietly to herself, "The youngster's *name* is Mark." She glanced at me with a surreptitious smile and a wink. Then she and Dad left quietly, and I watched from my bed as they disappeared down the hall and around the corner.

That first night was not at all pleasant. After Mom and Dad left, the nurses came back to draw more blood. They were not very nice about explaining things to me, but they were fervently committed to their mission, holding me down and locking my arms and legs. It really didn't require much effort, as I had little ability to move my extremities of my own volition, so their measures seemed like overkill. I told them I would be brave and cooperate, but they were in too much of a hurry and also said they would need to do this again tomorrow.

I lay awake through most of the night, listening to all of the noises and ominously beeping machines. They were like metronomes, monotonously droning the tempo of life. Sirens wailed outside. The passing lights made shadows flicker on the ceiling.

I was so young, I did not have all the words I needed to describe how I was feeling, so I often used just one. From an early age, I had sometimes found myself submerged by a strong cocktail of emotions. There was anxiety mixed with melancholy and a touch of fear and loneliness. There was also a splash of doom, where it seemed there was nothing to look forward to and no one to look forward with—a sense of void or emptiness. Lacking a more extensive vocabulary,

I had learned to label this feeling as "turtles." There was no rhyme or reason for this, and the term had nothing to do with actual reptiles. It was just a word chosen by a small boy to label and compartmentalize a complex set of overwhelming feelings.

That first night in Lakewood Hospital, the "turtles" feeling washed over me like a rogue wave. Seemingly abandoned by my parents, I could only lie there and wonder, *What if the doctors and nurses can't fix me? Will I be broken forever?*

Much to my relief, Mom and Dad returned at four o'clock the following day. In an effort to perk me up, Dad told me he had a surprise and handed me a brightly wrapped box. I had some difficulty opening it because of my weakened hands, but eventually managed to reveal its contents: two official-looking, US Army–style walkie-talkies, green with red buttons on the sides—the "something special" they had told me about. We set them up, inserting new batteries, and Dad took one out of the room and down the hall.

We tried to converse but I didn't have enough strength in my hand to depress the red transmitter button with my thumb. I tried repeatedly, then with both hands, but to no avail. I was brokenhearted. My parents seemed noticeably concerned, too, but Dad recovered quickly, offering one of his pithy aphorisms about having a positive attitude. He would return them to the store, he said, and by the time I was better they would probably come out with a better model.

Clearly something is seriously wrong, but what? Why do I feel so weak?

The next day, the doctor supervising my case told us that they were planning to do a lumbar puncture. He explained that this was a procedure to sample cerebral spinal fluid, the coating around my spinal cord. This would allow them to confirm the diagnosis if it revealed the presence of specific antibodies and immune cells. He suspected I had somehow contracted a disease called Guillain-Barré syndrome, or GBS.

Less common in children than adults, GBS is a neurological disease where the body's own immune system manufactures antibodies that attack the conductive coating or sheath, called myelin, around the peripheral nerves. It's like losing portions of an electric wire that conduct a current to a lamp or appliance. Without the protective, conductive covering, the electrical current is impeded or blocked altogether. As a result, function of the arms and legs, facial movements, and even breathing are affected. In some instances, the result can be death.

In an effort to sound hopeful, the doctor said there were some therapeutic measures known to help, but it would take some time before we knew the extent of my disease. He also assured us that he was consulting with doctors from another hospital where they'd seen more cases.

"At this time, we do not have a specific cure," the doctor told my parents. "But many patients spontaneously improve—some to normalcy—after several weeks, or occasionally months." However, he went on, because my breathing was increasingly impaired, I might need to use an iron lung.

There was hardly any time to take all this in before I was being prepped for the lumbar puncture. Mom and Dad were told to wait outside my room without even being given time to kiss me goodbye. Dad winked from the doorway as they left.

"Be tough, pal."

I was turned on my side as nurses at the head and foot of the bed restrained any movement of my hands or feet. Someone else held my head still from both sides. My heart was pounding and racing as though it might burst right out of my chest, but I was too weak to even begin resisting. My biggest fear was of the unknown. I did not know what to expect. Everyone seemed to be talking at once—to each other but not to me. I kept asking for someone to please explain what was happening but got no answer. The fear and anxiety kept mounting.

Doctors began placing green towels over my entire body except for my lower back. This raised my core temperature and further increased the perspiration produced by my distress. My lips began to quiver, and I could taste the salt in my sweat and the occasional tears.

Suddenly someone was pouring cold liquid all over my back and scrubbing with a brush of some kind. Then a female voice warned, "This may feel a little cold."

A male voice followed. "Now you might feel a slight—"

And with that, a stabbing needle stick caused a sudden burst of air to be expelled from my lungs before the man finished his sentence with the purely descriptive word "pinch."

"Is it over?" I cried out. "Is that it?"

"Almost," the man somewhere behind me answered. "The medicine I injected will numb the area so you don't feel the longer puncture needle and catheter as it goes in, okay?" *Say what?* He paused a moment, then added, "Here we go . . ."

With that, a penetrating sensation flared throughout my lower back. An electric shock seemed to travel from my back to my head and toes simultaneously. I screamed for them to stop and please let me go. I didn't think I could take a moment more, but the pain persisted as they held me still. Finally I heard, "I think we have enough fluid. We're finished, Mark. You did really well."

The relief turned out to be short-lived. I was told that although the fluid volume was adequate, repeating the procedure was the best way of monitoring progress of the disease. I would have to endure this procedure again at another hospital.

5

WATER

High in the 11 West tower at Metro, time seemed to be suspended. The minutes, hours, and days following the fire blurred together into one continuous moment of pain, grief, and exhaustion. Having survived the critical first forty-eight hours, I faced the first steps on my long road to recovery seemingly alone, clueless as to how desolate and torturous it would be.

Making the journey harder was the absence of clear direction and seemingly little information about the route. From my perspective, doctors rarely had the time to explain things to me.

The sense of being at their mercy was exacerbated by my inability to speak. The breathing tube literally choked off any attempt to form words. The state of my arms and hands, swollen like tree trunks and with bulky dressings, meant that sign language was all but impossible.

Frequently I'd find myself on the edge of panic, brimful with anxiety at being left alone in such agony yet unable to communicate my needs to the nurse. I did find one way to get her attention, but it did not endear me to her or the medical staff. Trying to remove the breathing tube from my throat, I hyperextended my head and neck. I failed to pull the tube free but managed to disconnect it from a longer piece that attached to the ventilator. This resulted in setting off a distress alarm at the nursing station, which usually brought one of the nurses to the room stat.

At some stage during those first days a speech therapist brought a letter board to my bedside. The idea was that I would point to the large letters, spelling out what I wanted to say, but lifting my swollen arms and holding my hands steady enough to point out the right letters was a Herculean task. Plus, severe facial swelling and a constant flow of tears meant that most of the time I was unable to clearly see the letters on the board.

Despite the barriers in expressive communication, I usually found ways to state the obvious or indicate that I was in immense pain. But there were also barriers in receptive communication. In the first few days I didn't realize the nurses were giving me medication intravenously to ease my pain, because I wasn't actually seeing the injections. The fact that I didn't experience any real relief only compounded my fear that little was being done. Eventually I understood the meaning of "IV" and "We're giving you something for the pain." Regardless, no amount of medication could alleviate the discomfort of a major burn.

Dressing changes, which were done once during each eight-hour shift, especially on critical patients, were a major

PTSD-inducing ordeal. They are the most labor-intensive and emotionally exhausting procedures for both patient and caregiver. The nurses would routinely premedicate me with a bolus of morphine, but never enough to make me relax or affect a noticeable decrease in pain as the procedure itself was hyperstimulating, especially to exposed nerve endings. Efforts by staff to ease my pain were also tempered by their fears of suppressing my breathing with higher doses of narcotics.

While seemingly prudent in theory, this "safe" practice has rarely proven clinically beneficial, as the intensity of pain itself generally overrides any degree of respiratory suppression. In fact, throughout this and most other procedures patients typically exhibit increased heart rate, blood pressure, and respiratory rate. Some practitioners now are more liberal with pain medication, their actions being supported by scientific evidence. But ask any burn patient and they'll say it's never enough. There's nothing so painful as a large burn injury—not even childbirth.

In response to thermal injuries, the body's immune system produces a soupy fluid called exudate, which saturates dressings within hours of their application. Therefore, one of the primary aspects of burn care is changing the topical creams, ointments, and medicated gauze bandages. With patients as physiologically unstable as I was, the procedure is usually done at the bedside by the primary nurse with assistants helping to position extremities or move patients from side to side. This also allows the staff to change bed linens while old drainage-soaked bandages are removed.

The entire process might consume three hours. Every aspect of the procedure, especially burn wound cleansing, was immensely painful and anticipated with great dread. Like most burn patients, I could become combative, uncooperative, and exhausted. This only further contributed to the overall stress.

After removal of adherent dressings, my burns were cleansed with Betadine, an antimicrobial similar to iodine that burned with topical application. Once all the wounds had been washed or scrubbed—each step making me shriek—they then had to be covered with fresh dressings. So from that point every step had to be performed under near-sterile conditions.

First, a nurse would need to scrub thoroughly, don a sterile gown and gloves, and open all dressings, ointments, and instruments onto a sterile draped table. Then an assistant would don sterile gloves and a gown as if preparing for surgery.

Betadine, which caused a merciless burning sensation, was also frequently utilized in an ointment form to inhibit bacterial growth. It was applied topically to the burns and caused a discomfort that lasted well after the dressing change.

Before application of the sterile bandages, the nurses or doctors would physically debride the burns of any loose or dying tissue, which included cutting or scraping of nonviable skin and tissue exudate. Sometimes the doctors would also cut away a small part of the wound to send for pathology studies or to rule out infection.

While all this was going on, a phlebotomist and nurses would simultaneously be sticking me with various needles: blood samples had to be drawn from veins beneath unburned skin, at different sites each time. Thus, multiple needle sticks were usually required. I came to dread the approach of each shift change, knowing what was coming.

Then there were procedures I didn't even have time to brace myself for. Just when one treatment or test ended it was time for something else. Because I was flat on my back for so long, at risk for pulmonary infections, the doctors were keeping a close eye on my breathing. Orders for another chest X-ray meant rolling me from side to side so a cold, sharp, metal film plate could be slid under me, cutting into my burned back.

One night, sometime after midnight, my temperature spiked to a worrisome 103 degrees. Fever of any kind suggested a potentially dangerous infection. The nurse on duty called the chief resident doctor, who was concerned that the burns on my upper arms had looked suspicious on rounds earlier that day. As a result, my newly applied dressings had to be removed again for the doctors to get a fresh look, despite having been changed only an hour before the temperature spike.

Daily weighing of my body, an important way to monitor my fluid levels, was an additional assault. I had to be rolled onto my side so that a plinth could be wedged under my body. Then I was pushed back onto it while clamps were attached to each corner, effectively making it a giant scale. A hydraulic lift would raise the frame with me on it, and once my weight had been recorded, the whole process had to be reversed to get me back into bed. Each shift of position brought compressing pressures that further angered my already tender wounds. And always sooner than later it would be time for another dressing change.

As if the burns themselves were not enough, over time I also began to develop pressure sores on my lower hip, tailbone, and right heel, caused by prolonged weight bearing and resultant decreased blood flow. Often these ulcers were more painful than the burns. In their efforts to prevent further development of pressure sores, the nurses would come in every twenty to thirty minutes and roll me to a new position, relieving pressure in one area in exchange for another and causing the pain to flare up all over. But even with such preventative care, pressure sores still occurred.

The complete lack of control, as I was endlessly pushed, prodded, and pinched, was somehow made worse by the seemingly brisk way in which the nurses performed many routine tasks. They moved from one body part to the next with incredible haste, as though they were late for a train. No sooner had I breathed a sigh of relief as the trauma in one part of my body subsided than they were on to the next. With hardly time to catch my breath—or for the ventilator to provide one—the cutting and poking moved to another part of my body. I was constantly caught off guard, frequently mistaking their efficiency for indifference.

All of this only added to my inner turmoil. I was still reeling from the grief of losing Mom and Toby. I was fearful for what might be the long-term consequences of my injuries. My heart broke for Dad as I saw the brave face he tried to project during his visits, a determination to encourage me that only made me feel worse for somehow having failed him by not protecting the family.

And now I was on an emotional roller coaster with regard to those caring for me. I'd be angry and combative, struggling when their attentions caused me pain. Sometimes it felt like I was fighting them, trying to defend myself: the body will instinctively do whatever it can to avoid pain, even when the pain is being caused with good intentions.

At the end of a major dressing change I would often be tearful and emotionally drained. The pain was so exhausting and exasperating that it was nearly impossible to keep my feelings in check. Though I could not communicate clearly because of being intubated, anyone could tell by my manner and facial expressions that I was angry, sad, or simply distraught and guilt-ridden.

At the same time, my anger would be splashed with fear that I might have driven a wedge between myself and the caregivers on whom I depended. I worried that my outbursts or strangled cries of desperation might cause the nurses to dislike me, making them less gentle-handed during the next dressing change. This fear that an ally could also be an adversary was likely a psychological holdover from my early childhood when I battled GBS.

Just when it felt like I could not take any more, I was given a moment's relief. One day early in the journey, I had been through a particularly trying dressing change in which I battled the doctors and nurses each step of the way. We all seemed relieved when it was finally completed. I felt shame and guilt for the way I had treated everyone. Though I couldn't talk clearly, I tried to make amends through my facial expressions and gestures. The nurse assigned to me for the day was named Helen. She had dark hair and warm, soft eyes. She moved more closely to the bed.

"It's okay, baby," she said tenderly, with a smile in her eyes. "You've been through a lot, but it's going to get better." Then she leaned over the bed rail and kissed me gently on the forehead. A soothing calm seemed to flow across my skin and deep into my chest.

Alone with my thoughts, I spent long hours replaying what had happened at the house that night of August 3, questioning what I might have done differently and wondering why God had allowed things to go the way they did. At times I'd also wonder whether he really existed. I'd mull over these thoughts as I looked out the exterior window of my room, the Cleveland sky usually as gray and gloomy as I felt.

Though I was in constant, grinding pain, during those first few weeks I never lost a desperate desire for water. From the moment I awoke in the ambulance, I felt parched, as though I'd die of thirst. I had not been allowed anything by mouth—not even a drop. The yearning never left me for one second. *Water!* I had a raging thirst and ached for some refreshment.

I'd beg the nurses, attempting and failing to verbalize the word "water" around the ventilator tube or through pointing out the letters on a board. But I had been told adamantly I could not have anything orally. The nurses tried to explain that in my condition the risks associated with swallowing even a sip of fluid were too great. Because of the ventilator tube, any fluids spilling into the lungs could result in a fatal pneumonia—surprisingly one of the most common causes of death among burn patients.

So I fantasized. I imagined the sensation of cool drops splashing onto my lips and tongue. When one of the nurses or other staff would tell me they were breaking for lunch or dinner, I would visualize every aspect of their meal. Sipping, tasting, and chewing become prized activities when you are denied their usual joys for an extended period.

Relief came on my ninth day in the burn intensive care unit (BICU). Through the interior window of my room that looked out on the central nurses' station, I saw a large group of white-coated men and women emerge from the elevators at the end of the hall. The senior doctors had arrived to conduct their "grand rounds" with some junior residents and trainee staff.

I was familiar with these visits. They usually occurred in the early morning hours before scheduled surgeries, or at the end of the day after all operations had been completed. Typically, the group would gather outside a room to discuss the status of its patient. Led by the attending physician, this briefing could last from five to thirty minutes. Then everyone would squeeze into the patient's room, where any necessary examinations or questioning would be completed within just a minute or two.

Sometimes these grand rounds were made spontaneously in the middle of the day at the whim of the doctor in charge. Such a visit took place that afternoon when I was selected as the subject to be displayed for the residents and students. As a result, all of my dressings had to be removed again so that a dozen pairs of eyes could closely examine my wounds.

With the memory of the morning's painful dressing change still fresh, I was wary when the group entered my room. Leading the way was a rather rotund man with black and gray hair balding on top, and a mustache like a wire brush with salt and pepper flecks. He wore thick-framed glasses and his lab coat breast pocket was loaded with pens, a flashlight, and measuring devices. Like kangaroo pouches, the larger side pockets contained a collection of folded papers and lists, paperback manuals, and a black stethoscope.

As the chief resident leading the group, he spoke with a triumphant tone. "We've got good news and bad," he announced, causing me to prick up my ears in expectation and concern. "The bad news is that you're going to be going to surgery tomorrow. It will be the first of many surgeries you'll need before going home. We'll be debriding your burns under general anesthesia, so you'll be asleep."

Surgery didn't sound good, but the prospect of going home did.

"The good news," he continued, "is that you won't have to feel anything, because we'll be doing all of your dressing changes while you sleep. If all goes well you may not need your arm dressings changed for another five days."

This was indeed positive progress! But there was more.

"Also, tonight we're going to pull that tube from your throat to see how well you breathe on your own without the ventilator."

He paused, adding cautiously, "If you do well, we may allow you to have sips of clear liquids, beginning with ice chips, and maybe progressing to thirty milliliter sips each hour. However, we will need to replace the tube for surgery, and it may need to stay in a while after the operation. We'll be back after rounds to pull the tube."

Never mind that thirty milliliters was only about the size of a shot glass. The anticipation was intense. For the first time in as long as I could remember, something like delight flooded through me. The thought of cool, clear water trickling down my raw, parched throat left me ecstatic.

I was giddy, so busy savoring what lay ahead that I didn't take in much of what the chief resident went on to explain to the rest of the group clustered around my bed.

This first surgery, he told them, was to perform a more extensive debridement of all of my burns. Having me under general anesthesia would allow the doctors to go deeper. The procedure would likely cause a significant amount of blood loss, and up until this point I had not been physiologically stable enough to tolerate the stress of such a demanding surgery.

In fact, I was still at some risk for cardiac arrhythmias, among other complications including infection and a potential blood loss resulting in low blood pressure that could lead to shock. Even death was a possibility, but they did not want to wait much longer before starting my recovery process. The deeper, full thickness burns, especially those on my hands, arms, and legs, were not going to heal without skin grafts.

The grafting surgery, to be planned for another day, would involve taking skin from unburned areas of my body and transferring it to the areas with deeper burns. This would then essentially leave new wounds, much like additional burns, in the donor sites where the replacement skin was harvested. Tomorrow's surgery, the doctor in charge explained, was primarily about preparing the burns for later grafting by clearing away all dead and damaged tissue.

If they were able to debride the burns adequately, they might use temporary pigskin to cover the deeper burns. This would buy extra time for the burns to begin the healing process. It was only a temporary measure, however, because my body's immune system would start to reject the pigskin after a week or two. By that time, though, if things had gone well, I might be able to tolerate grafting of my own skin. In any event, the chief resident restated, this would be the first of many surgeries I would require before I was well enough to think about going home.

After the bearer of my good news departed with his students and junior residents in tow, other doctors adjusted the ventilator so that the number of automatic breaths it delivered would be gradually tapered off through the course of the afternoon.

I was essentially breathing on my own by the time the chief resident and his group returned a few hours later with a respiratory therapist right behind them. The chief stood at the head of my bed and disconnected my tube from where it attached to the ventilator. He leaned over me so that I stared directly at his upside-down face, his bushy mustache poking out from behind a loosely hanging surgical mask. His stethoscope dangled like a pendulum over my projecting chin and neck.

"On the count of three, ready?" he said. "One, two, and three!"

It felt like I was coughing up a wire hairbrush, and a series of loud hacks produced gobs of black sputum. When the coughing finally stopped, Helen, the nurse, placed a soft green plastic mask over my nose and mouth. It had a unique scent as the cool sensation of 100 percent pure oxygen flooded my nostrils. I was euphoric to be breathing on my own without help from the machine, although my throat felt like it had been scraped raw.

The promise of water filled every fiber of my being. As Helen brought the first spoonful of ice chips toward my lips, my whole body seemed to quiver with anticipatory chills.

"Go slowly," she cautioned as everything in me strained to move toward the white plastic spoon. Its edge gently nudged the tip of my tongue.

Anyone who says water has no taste has not gone without enjoying its splendor for any length of time. As Helen carefully held the spoon out, my olfactory nerves fired in a fusillade of synapses. I could detect the scent of the minerals within the frozen chips, accompanied by a slight tingle that I would forever after associate with the pleasant fragrance of plastic.

The ice fragments released a soft breeze of frost that wafted past my dilating nostrils, causing the gentle trickle of an involuntary salty tear. As the crystalline diamonds spilled onto my tongue, I reflexively contracted it to form a long trough, capturing the ice pieces to savor for as long as possible.

The intensity was incredible. I let the sensations wash over me as I absorbed every drop. Such a simple moment, yet it seemed like the most complex span of seconds as I thanked God for the delightful banquet. I couldn't help but marvel at what an amazing experience it was to simply taste and swallow a few ice chips. It may have only been a few drops, but it seemed to awaken something deep inside me. The experience of such pleasure after a period of unending pain somehow gave birth to a new sensation—hope. It was the first time since the fire that I was able to see some light beyond the veil of despair that hung around and over me.

Somehow those sips reminded me of what I had believed for so long: there was definitely a Divine Being out there, someone in charge—and maybe he did care after all.

"Thank you, God," I murmured. I knew that I'd remember this moment forever.

The respiratory therapist, Kathy, stayed with me that evening, helping me to cough up and expel as much phlegm and blackened sputum as possible between sips. It seemed my thirst could never be slaked, nor could the rawness of my throat be relieved.

With short, steel-colored hair, soft facial features, and powder-blue eyes, Kathy was warm and gentle, exuding an assuring confidence and easygoing nature. She told me that she was a single mom of two daughters near my age. She asked if I was nervous about surgery the next day and the possibility of waking up with the breathing tube back in.

Being able to speak again was great, though my throat was so sore and my voice scratchy. Hoarse and halting, I told Kathy that I was pretty scared by the possibility of not waking up at all, though the prospect of waking up with the tube back in had me extremely anxious if not terrified.

Quietly she asked, "Do you believe in God? Do you think that he knows and loves everyone and has a plan for each and every one of us?"

The questions came casually, easily, but they took me by surprise. Kathy had given voice to the very thing I had been wrestling with over the past few hours. I told her how I desperately wanted to believe it. But how could a loving God's plan include losing some of my family and being horribly burned? It just didn't make any sense.

Kathy reached over the bed railing and gently touched my cheek.

"God has something really special planned for you, Mark," she said. "There's a reason you survived. And in his perfect world, there's a reason for everything."

Her care and sincerity struck a chord. Her gentle tone touched me deeply. Tears welled up, and I wished I could just reach out for a hug, to cry on her shoulder.

Kathy told me she'd be keeping a close eye on me in the coming days, and that she and her girls would pray for me as I went through the surgery.

"Keep the faith, Mark," she said. "Trust God. He loves you. He has a plan for you—even if you don't understand it right now."

6

RAINBOW

It wasn't the first time I'd lain in a hospital bed wondering where God was and why he had let these things happen. Ten years earlier I had wrestled with similar thoughts and feelings. And that was at an age when I was even less equipped to understand the implications of complex concepts such as mortality and death.

The seriousness of my GBS became clearer as I was being transported from Lakewood Hospital to Rainbow Babies and Children's Hospital, known locally as Rainbow or RB&C, on Cleveland's east side. With a stellar reputation, its medical team included the famous author and pediatrician Benjamin Spock, and Frederick C. Robbins, a 1954 recipient of the Nobel Prize in Physiology or Medicine for research in developing the life-saving polio vaccine.

On the way in the ambulance, I again found it difficult to breathe—something that had been occurring more frequently. I couldn't seem to get deep enough breaths. As they became progressively more shallow, the EMTs had me breathe with the aid of a special mask. This kind of supplemental oxygen would become mandatory over the next several days.

My struggles to breathe became so labored that doctors decided there was no other option but to place me in a negative pressure ventilator (an iron lung) to help my weakened chest muscles. They called it my spaceship in an effort to ease my anxiety, but there was no way around the utter fear of being placed inside. Lying in a body-sized can with my head sticking out through a hole at one end, I resembled a Pez dispenser.

It was understandable that my thoughts turned to dying, or as close as my mind could venture to such a difficult concept: the fear of being abandoned by my parents. I would count the minutes until they arrived at visiting time, then count down the minutes until they had to leave again.

When Dad came he would often take a break from his usual bedside attendance and walk down to the hospital cafeteria for a cup of coffee or a snack. I became so afraid of the possibility that he might not return—or worse, have no reason to return because my condition might have further deteriorated—that I would ask him to leave his watch with me. It had a square face with a brown leather band, and I would hold it close or set it on my bedside table in direct view. It was not as though some part of me really doubted Dad would come back. I had implicitly trusted him ever since our faith exercises of early childhood in the dark basement. But having such an expensive and personal possession of his offered some sort of further assurance.

Some tasks were simply too painful, like opening a milk carton. I'd have to wait until a nurse came in or passed my door and then politely ask for help, despite regretting the need to do so. It didn't take much to find myself on the verge of tears. And I would wonder, *What did I do wrong for all this to happen to me?*

Growing up I had been taught that death was synonymous with living eternally and happily in God's presence. That belief was somewhat comforting as far as it went, but it was all still a bit mysterious.

During my elementary school years I served as an altar boy, assisting the priests with Mass celebrations on Sundays and even weekdays during Lent. Dad was a commentator, helping with Scripture readings during Sunday Mass; but as we boys grew older, weekly attendance became less rigid. Some of my understanding of the nature of God stemmed from the teachings of Catholicism, including that he is omnipotent, omnipresent, and omniscient. From the Bible and the influence of others, I believed that Jesus died as payment for my sins and that he was the way to salvation and heaven.

From here on, things were rather opaque. Being raised Catholic, I would go to confession, although as I grew older I was never really clear about the difference between mortal and venial sins—whether I was in danger of total or partial loss of grace, respectively. The idea of penance didn't make much sense to me either, as it seemed to distract from the value of such a sacrifice on God's part. Surely, either God forgave me or he didn't. If I was thinking about stealing a candy bar from the local store, did I have to weigh in my mind that it might cost me twenty Hail Marys?

Finding myself at Rainbow left me facing questions that I could not formulate clearly, much less hope to answer. Like any child of similar age, I saw things in black and white, everything with a direct cause and effect.

Being critically ill made me wonder if I had done something wrong. *Somehow, the painful things that are happening must be my fault.* A dark cloud hung over me. *Am I responsible for my condition? And if the disease is not curable, am I going to die?*

Just the thought of being separated from my parents, let alone God, was mortifying. No wonder I did what I could to ensure that I was not abandoned by the closest representation of God I knew on earth: my father. He and Mom continued to encourage me to have faith and be strong. Alone at night, I'd try to remember their words, asking God to help me and make me well even as the fears and uncertainties bubbled below the surface.

Time seemed to slow down at Rainbow. I viewed the medical teams as assassins wielding stainless steel instruments or wheeling some machine, contraption, or cart stocked with what I thought of as their implements of torture. I'd be restrained in leather cuffs, straps, and buckles, forced into submission, not really understanding how the awful things they were doing to me were supposed to help.

My nutritional status was also compromised, and as a result I was losing weight. Physical therapy was instituted to maintain my range of motion and try to stimulate any and all types of muscle function while improving my appetite.

Gradually, over the course of several weeks, my increasing ability to breathe on my own allowed me to spend less time in the "spaceship." I graduated to an oxygen tent, where the concentrations were decreased day by day. It was difficult for me to appreciate the improvement, but the doctors and nurses seemed to agree that these were objective signs of nerves beginning to work again and evidence of the healing process.

Slowly, I began to notice volitional movement in my extremities. Progress was not without setbacks, however. One particular day in the therapy gym, nothing seemed to be in my favor and the most minor of challenges seemed to sap all my limited energy stores. Just getting bathed and dressed with someone assisting me left me exhausted. I wanted to cry, if not scream for mercy.

As part of my rehabilitation, my physical therapist, Miss Sheryl, helped to advance my legs in the parallel bars, though it seemed to me I was hanging by my armpits. I must have resembled a marionette with spaghetti noodles for strings. I recall one time she gradually "guided" my plunge to the floor with a stern glare that seemed devoid of sympathy. As we sat on the floor, she remained impassive to my pleading "help me" stare.

Finally, after I summoned the energy to make the smallest effort to lift myself, she began to speak. She explained to me the difference between sympathy and empathy, smiling all the while with warm eyes that reflected her true nature, one of constant encouragement. I didn't recognize it at the time as my first lesson in tough love.

The physical, occupational, and speech therapists began working with me more consistently two and three times daily. Speech therapists taught me proper techniques in swallowing, which helped me to breathe again through my mouth while speaking.

Sessions involved a tilt table to address some of the most neurologically debilitating symptoms of GBS, such as loss of balance and bodily awareness. The tilt table brought my body to an upright position gradually after being horizontal for so long. This prevented me from losing consciousness due to a sudden drop in blood pressure. It felt strange to be learning to walk all over again, and it was days before I could simply be upright without dizziness. And I still had little control over my balance; it would be weeks before I could walk across a room without feeling as though I'd just stepped off a merry-go-round.

Finally, one evening while the medical team was making rounds, we received the long-awaited news that I would be discharged at the end of the week. I could continue rehabilitation as an outpatient. I felt a rush of relief and excitement and then a twinge of apprehension. I didn't want to stay in the hospital anymore, but I had become used to being there. I wondered how well I'd function at home without daily help from the nurses. I was also fearful about returning to school, so it was a relief to be excused from kindergarten to undergo therapy, although state law required me to repeat that grade the following year.

My endurance was slowly improving, yet sometimes the drive to or from the hospital was as exhausting as the hour-long therapy sessions. Those months filled with moments of encouragement from my mother were the seeds of some of my fondest memories, however. I would lie across the front seat of Mom's car with my head in her lap, in the days before wearing seat belts was compulsory. I recall the texture of her navy and green plaid wool skirt rough against my cheek. I can still see her bobby-socked feet in penny loafers, working the gas and brake pedals. She would frequently multitask, applying lipstick and rouge while scratching my head lightly. She'd be smiling and humming, or we'd sing songs together like Simon and Garfunkel's "Bridge over Troubled Water."

7

AUGUST 13, 1976

In the wake of unspeakable pain, the simplest pleasures are somehow even sweeter. After surfing waves of agony for ten days, I was craving a drink to slake my raging thirst. That first evening I was permitted sips of water was like a trip to an oasis.

I wondered about what Kathy had said to me regarding God and his care or plan for me. I was still unclear and uncertain, even as I thanked him for the joy of refreshing liquid. And then, all too soon, it was time to head back out into the desert.

As a standard precaution, patients are not allowed to drink or eat anything eight hours before surgery. The NPO rule—*nil per os*, which is Latin for "nothing by mouth"—is intended to keep stomach contents from getting into the lungs and increasing the chance of infection should the patient become nauseated and vomit.

I desperately wanted some more water when Dad appeared in my room at 6:00 a.m., along with two orderlies ready to take me to surgery. Before they wheeled me off, Dad leaned over and kissed me on the forehead.

"We'll be praying for you, chum," he said, trying to be bright. "We'll be right here when you get back." There was a quiver to his usual upbeat tone. I could tell that he was holding back tears. We shared a brief silence before I was transferred to a gurney for my ride. No words were necessary as we looked into each other's eyes.

The orderlies and nurses made sure that the railings on both sides of the bed were raised and locked in place.

"It's a long, bumpy ride through the tunnels of the hospital," said one of the orderlies, who introduced himself as Roosevelt. "We'd sure hate to lose you before we get to surgery!" He grinned, his eyes bright behind black spectacles. Roosevelt was cheery, making it seem as if he were escorting me to a party rather than a serious operation.

We took the elevator to the sub-basement, emerging into what appeared to be a makeshift tunnel, which Roosevelt said was a temporary detour around never-ending new construction. Lined with walls of plywood and supported with two-by-fours, it reminded me of an old mine shaft. A slight sickly yellow glow washed from the temporary sodium lights hanging in overhead wire cages.

The burns on my back stung with every bump on the irregular floor. As we trundled along, Roosevelt explained the different colored stripes on the uneven cement, perhaps trying to distract me from the discomfort. The markings were coded guidelines pointing the way through the tunnels to various destinations throughout the hospital complex. It was all very confusing to me; I could imagine Hansel and Gretel getting lost down there, even with an endless supply of bread crumbs marking their trail.

It was busy, an underground city full of noises and voices and occasional drafts of cold air. People bustled in all directions. Some were in different colored scrubs, others wore white lab coats. There were fellow patients, some in wheelchairs, others on gurneys.

Then we passed a small booth, also constructed of two-by-fours and plywood, where a man stood selling newspapers, magazines, candy, and snacks. Roosevelt explained that it was known as the "blind stand" since the vendor was blind and patrons were on their honor to provide the correct change for their purchases.

Every time we encountered bumps along the cement corridors my wounds were jarred. I groaned and winced despite my escorts' best efforts to give me a smooth ride. Finally, after twenty minutes or so, Roosevelt wheeled me into another elevator that rose to the third floor, where the doors opened to a peculiar sign: "Restricted to Appropriate Personnel and Attire."

Inside, our trio was swamped by a passel of nurses and doctors. It was amazing to see so much activity, like New York City's Grand Central Station during rush hour. I was aware of other patients nearby in the preoperative area. They also were being prepped for surgery behind curtain dividers that barely offered some measure of privacy. An anesthesiologist introduced himself as the person who would ensure my comfort during the operation. He began probing my extremities for the access he told me they needed.

Oh no, I thought. *More prodding and needle sticks. I feel like I'm a human pincushion. Can't they wait till I'm asleep?* Around me other members of the team were asking each other questions, making notes on charts, and looking busy and efficient.

Stark brightness greeted me in the operating room, where I was positioned alongside the single table in the center. Three large circular lights, like flying saucers, were suspended from the ceiling. Several people in scrubs, paper hats, and masks scurried in, out, and around the room. Their feet were covered with paper slippers, causing them to pitter-patter across the floor. Everyone seemed to be talking at once, their voices echoing off the walls. It was frigid—so cold I thought it might snow. Using the bedsheets like a sling, several orderlies hoisted me up from the gurney and positioned me on the operating table. It was cold and hard—ominously like a slab in some morgue, it occurred to me, probably from watching too many police shows. My head was positioned on a silicone ring they called a "donut." It was surprisingly comfortable to my scalp. To the side, I could see large tables draped with green sheets and lined with a monstrous display of stainless steel instruments.

I could feel my heart beginning to race. That medicine I had been given earlier to relax me did not seem to be working!

Then the anesthesiologist was back, standing at my head. "You're going to be going off to sleep now, Mark," he said in a matter-of-fact tone. "And when you wake up again, the surgery will be finished. You won't feel anything; we'll take good care of you."

I followed his instructions to begin counting backwards from one hundred, though with my throat still raw and hoarse I could manage only a raspy whisper.

"One hundred, ninety-nine, ninety-eight, ninety-seven," I began. My eyelids grew heavy, seemingly weighted with lead. My head felt heavier. Everything was pulling me down into nothingness.

I had no idea how long it lasted, but then awareness came abruptly. I was yanked into consciousness by a terrible burning sensation traveling from my stomach up to my chest and neck. A flare across my belly caused my abdominal muscles to contract involuntarily. It was the kind of reflex spasm that occurs from being tickled, only this one was much stronger and it was all a gripping pain. I felt awake but could not open my eyes.

Next, I felt cutting or peeling down in my abdominal region. It was a curious but horrifying sensation. I was aware of my abdominal muscles slowly contracting into a frozen spasm, one I was powerless to prevent, as though a massive boa constrictor was coiled around my stomach, squeezing the life out of me.

Then came the unmistakable but at the same time unfathomable sharp sensation of something sawing back and forth across my stomach. *What is happening?* It was an icy-cold burning, like tearing skin from the base of my cuticles but over my whole body. I was being skinned alive! I would have been writhing on the table if not for the fact that I was paralyzed.

I tried to scream out loud but found that I could not utter a sound. I could hear voices, muffled words from the shuffling of people around me. *Oh yes,* I remembered. *The operating table. I am in surgery. Perhaps I am dreaming. Maybe this is some kind of nightmare. I must not be quite asleep or quite awake.*

But as more pain assaulted my body, I realized with horror it was much worse. *I am awake! The anesthesia hasn't taken properly!*

Again, I tried desperately to scream out loud, but my body would not obey my mind's direction to cry for help. I simply could not move my lips and still couldn't open my eyes. I was unable to voluntarily twitch a muscle. My head was pounding, throbbing like a kick drum, so much that I thought it might explode at any moment. I could hear the rapid beating of my heart, an ocean of pounding pulses somewhere deep behind my ears.

The figures around me were talking to one another. The words were not always decipherable—just jumbled, empty sounds from a distant, cavernous vacuum—but I could tell from the tone that there was no great sense of urgency or alarm. It was all quite businesslike.

Oh God, they don't know that I'm feeling all of this! They don't know that I am awake! Oh God, please let them realize . . .

The cutting and peeling sensation continued, the pain and terror building and building inside my head until I thought it was about to erupt like a volcano and spew my molten brain tissue around the room. My abdominal muscles continued their forceful, rhythmic contractions. The crushing spasms came as something cool and sharp sliced across my torso; I could feel it violently tearing away my skin.

Along with the steely pressure I could feel soft and icy stickiness rippling across my abdomen and washing down over my flanks, dripping like cold syrup—blood. The coppery smell could not belie its identity.

Then there was heat and the distinct, sickly sweet smell of burning flesh. *They must be trying to staunch the bleeding by cauterizing the burns*, I guessed, further incinerating the surface of my skin with a fusillade of electric shocks. *Oh God, not more burning; please stop the burning.*

Whoever was holding my arm must have then let go. All of a sudden it dropped like a stone over the side of the operating table, swinging like a pendulum as blood dripped from the torpid, powerless limb to the tile floor below. The torturous sensation momentarily distracted me from the relentless contracting of my abdomen. It was accompanied by a sharp grating, like someone scraping the inside of a bowl, only this was my stomach.

Pain, fear, and helplessness swirled around, welling up inside to where I thought I would implode and sink into a black hole, unreachable.

I am literally bleeding to death. At least this—death—will stop the pain.

Lying still and vulnerable—unable to twitch a muscle, blink an eye, or move in the slightest way despite my mind's frantic commands—was like being buried alive. *I cannot stand one more second of this agony. Surely no one could survive another second of this unbearable pain.* And then more seconds passed.

Words began to cut through the fog, though muddled and muffled as if coming from an adjacent room. "We're losing copious amounts of blood," I heard, clipped and urgent. "Where's it all coming from?"

My heart was pounding, my pulse was racing, and my blood pressure was spiraling down. But instead of exploding, my heart suddenly seemed to deflate. In an instant my body transitioned from a vat overflowing with turmoil to one draining away to nothing, as if someone had just pulled a plug. I was circling the drain.

"Pressure's low, let's hold up." *Did someone just say that? Oh yes, please stop.*

I'm dying, I accepted. *Please, God . . .*

A nd then suddenly, completely, wonderfully it was all over. Relief. The hurting stopped. I was pain-free, tranquil and peaceful, at rest. I seemed to be floating above my body, aware of a drama continuing somewhere below, people moving and speaking urgently. But it didn't really trouble me: I had never felt so happy, so content, and so calm.

I was lying on my back, facing the ceiling, with my knees bent at an angle, in just the sort of ideal position one would assume sprawled in a La-Z-Boy recliner. It was as though I was suspended on a pillow-cushion of air above the operating table, my arms at my sides. The air around me had gone from a cool, even chilling draft to a soothing blanket of warmth. It reminded me of relaxing on a sun-bathed beach with my eyes closed, while through their lids I was enjoying the gentle heat and radiant glow.

Though I was inexpressibly relaxed, my senses were humming at levels I had never before experienced. Instead of the torturous pain there was heightened visual and tactile awareness. Above all, I just knew, without really understanding how, that I was close to passing over some type of threshold.

Unconditional love, forgiveness, and acceptance flowed over me, a blanket of security and comfort. It was marvelous, yet the promise of even more seemed to build and build. If I continued drifting up the way I was going, toward the ceiling, I sensed I would pass into some unknown state of eternal love, bliss, euphoria—free of all worries or concerns. I was giddy with joy, aware of an urge to laugh out loud.

In the grip of pain just a few moments earlier, it had seemed like time stopped. Now I didn't want time to start, because that would mean this too would pass. I just wanted to linger in this blissful state beyond description. I didn't understand what was going on, but I had none of the anxiety commonly associated with things unknown.

Everything was just as it was intended to be. The world was perfectly aligned. All things—past, present, and yet to be—had a specific purpose and reason. My truth and existence resided in this moment. Everything was perfect, exactly as it was intended from the beginning of time, and would remain so forever.

And all of this was so plainly apparent that I felt like giggling at the simplicity and impeccability. *Oh . . . God! Of course! Who else?*

It was wonderful to be free from pain, but even that which I'd experienced did not matter anymore. And it was hard to even categorize it as bad. I knew that I had needed to suffer all of it in order to realize this current state of awareness. *No suffering is ever in vain. All pain has its purpose and is part of the plan.* The words of the old gospel song "Amazing Grace" came to mind: "Was blind, but now I see."

I wasn't actually looking with my eyes, but everything was coming into focus. My physical self was surrounded and suffused by soft light, an ethereal, luminous glow that caressed my body. As I moved slowly upward, the intensity of the brightness increased. Weightless and airy, I was thoroughly unconcerned with my physical existence. Whatever body I'd had up until now was merely a container for my real essence, my spirit, the true Mark.

My body, which had consumed so much attention from so many people over the past ten days, was of no ultimate consequence. In place of the physical, I had a heightened awareness of the metaphysical. I could almost smell and taste love, joy, peace, patience, kindness, goodness, faithfulness, gentleness, and self-control. I vaguely remembered once reading or hearing that in the Bible these characteristics, these essences, were called the fruit of the Spirit. Now I knew why. I could sense, even taste their sweet juices.

Beyond all this, I knew I was close to something, someone, immense and immeasurable. Someone in whose presence I felt loved, cherished, comforted, and protected was allowing me a sense of safety—complete bliss. It was God.

There were others around, angelic beings I could not see but somehow just knew were radiant, gentle, and strong. I could sense them guiding me, inviting me along a path of brilliant revelation.

Somewhere above, at least in my mind's eye, was a square-shaped tunnel ascending a gentle slope. Reclining comfortably, my body was gradually floating up toward the tunnel's peak. Somehow, I knew that the tunnel ended not much farther ahead and that to go beyond was to cross to some other side, to an existence no longer here but there, a place and reality I'd yet to know, where the light was brightest. The prospect was overwhelming, tantalizing, but not fearful. Yet, if this was an invitation it was not mine alone to accept.

Everything was so full, so complete, so as it should be that there didn't seem room for anything else. But then I became aware of something that amazed me further: Mom and Toby were there—here—with me. The sensation of their presence was like seeing, hearing, smelling, and touching them all at once.

I could not actually see them, but I knew they were present. There was no tangible physical sensation, but it was almost like Mom was holding my hand. Grandpa Larry, Dad's father who had died when I was a baby, was with us too. They didn't say anything, but I knew they were there to love me. I was excited, yet at the same time I also felt supremely calm.

It was as though I could see what I was feeling, and it was beautiful. This kind of new dimension went further. I seemed able to communicate thoughts or questions just through my mind. I didn't need to speak them; they were just heard. And the answers came from within me almost as soon as the questions were considered. I had a sense of omniscience: I just knew with a palpable certainty or clarity that provoked laughter and joy. The thirst for knowledge didn't exist, because the answers came faster than the desire for them—nothing to cause anxiety.

Of course! That makes so much sense! I would tell myself as each question and answer rose and fell. *It's the only way it could be!*

This certitude I was experiencing was pure, limitless joy. Everything was unequivocal; it was all in accordance with the grand scheme of things, part of God's perfect design and creation. *How did I miss this before?* It wasn't for lack of knowing; perhaps a deficiency of faith?

Holy God, I thought. *It's amazing . . . so amazing.*

It was a taste, a glimpse, a slice of heaven. But somehow I also knew it was just a fraction of all that heaven would allow.

As suddenly as I had found myself floating in this euphoric moment, I became aware of another truth—an incontestable reality. I could not remain where and as I was. Nor would I be passing over the threshold to what I perceived to be the preferred ultimate state of existence. It was not my time.

Again, without any words being spoken, I simply knew that I was needed at home with Dad and my brothers. I would survive the events in the operating room to continue my life with them. There would be much more pain to endure, but with God's help we'd survive that too. We would share our strength and our love, together enduring trials and whatever the future held.

Somehow I also knew that, just as Kathy had told me only hours before—*could it really have been so recently?*—I had a definite purpose in life, one that was yet to be fulfilled.

For now, Mom, Toby, and Grandpa Larry would wait. I had more living to do. And while it might not all be easy, I knew beyond a doubt that God would be with me all the way.

Then the comforting sleep that had eluded me wrapped me like a blanket.

8

TREE HOUSE

During those moments in the operating room—hovering between life and death, soaking in the certainty of meaning and purpose, confident in God's goodness and assured of the enduring love of lost loved ones—I had clarity about everything, an assurance beyond anything I had ever known.

Not that I hadn't tried previously to find the answers to all my questions. Like most teenagers, I had wrestled with who I was, who others wanted me to be, and what life was all about. That search had taken me along some paths I knew deep down weren't really going to lead me anywhere meaningful. But the scenery en route was good and some of my friends were along for the trip, so why not?

A tree house figured large in those wanderings.

I was about eight or nine when I came across a Cleveland newspaper clipping among some of Dad's memorabilia. He was featured in a story dating back to the late 1940s that addressed the housing shortage and economic stresses being felt in a postwar society. The article told how a group of teenagers—Dad and some of his best pals—had built a rather impressive tree house in the woods near his Bay Village home.

Illustrated with several photos, the article described the economically efficient project. Complete with a potbelly stove and electricity, the tree house had bunks for three, a small kitchen, a functioning door and windows, an exterior porch, and weather-resistant features such as insulation, tar paper, and a shingled roof.

Dad and his friends financed the construction with only a small portion of their college savings, which they had earned from paper routes, lawn mowing, and other entrepreneurial endeavors. Most of their supplies were scraps donated from various construction sites.

From the day I learned about Dad's project, I was enchanted if not obsessed. I wanted to build a tree house of comparable magnitude. I begged him for permission to construct one in the enormous weeping willow tree bordering our backyard. Adding weight to my petition was the fact that my best friend, Jeff, had recently persuaded his father to help build a platform in a willow in the backyard of their home in Bay Village—ironically, within a mile of where Dad had built his tree house some twenty years prior.

Eventually, one Saturday in September, Dad conceded. He agreed to help, but only with the first phase of the project. This gave him peace of mind that our additional construction would have a stable foundation. We took three two-by-fours, each about three feet long, and used long spikes to nail them horizontally across the tree trunk at their midpoints, the lowest one four feet above the ground, beyond the reach of toddlers. They were like free-floating ladder rungs that rose at three-foot intervals to a square platform.

The platform, though small, was just large enough for three or four of us to sit, perched high above the ground, beneath the canopy-like branches of the willow. Its shading branches were strings draping toward the ground like streamers of light exploding from fireworks on the Fourth of July. Plenty of sturdy branches allowed for future expansion.

That evening the air was brisk, with temperatures dropping to the mid-forties, quite chilly for early fall. Regardless, Paul Rattigan, Steve (another neighborhood friend), Tim, and I sat on our little platform for two or three hours, drinking hot chocolate and talking about life and how we'd build our tree house into a king's lair.

Soon we had four walls—one with a hinged, lockable door, another with a window—that together supported a roof with a trap door escape hatch.

The tree house would evolve over the coming years, with a large branch becoming the rustic central feature of the second story, which was also fully enclosed and accessible from the lower floor via the trap door. Two guys could sleep comfortably on each level. We also built a T-shaped porch extending out from the main door between two primary trunks of the tree. We added a railing onto the porch but enclosed the entire addition during winter months. Additionally, we built lookout platforms farther up in the tree, just like in *Swiss Family Robinson*.

Tucked away at the back of the property, the tree house afforded us a great deal of privacy with its walls and the cover of branches. As the central location for many youthful activities, unfortunately it also became the backdrop for some foolish ventures and the beginning days of experimenting with vices such as tobacco, pot, and alcohol.

Along with the tree house, the idyllic Bain Park where I hung out as a youngster would become the place to party as a teenager. Conveniently across the street from my house, it was the go-to meeting place throughout my junior and senior high school years.

One fall evening when I was in seventh grade, Dad accompanied me to a fathers-and-sons school presentation on sex. The weeknight event covered everything on reproduction, from fertilization to birth, in the most dry and boring manner. Understandably embarrassed, only a few of us attending raised our hands in the question-and-answer session that followed. I suspect most of us already knew the basics. On the way home, Dad asked if I had any questions. Awkwardly, I assured him that no, everything was cool: I already knew all about that stuff.

When the weekend rolled around, I asked for a ride to a friend's house. Dad promptly agreed and hurried us out to the car before the younger boys could ask to tag along. My curiosity turned to apprehension as he drove silently for the first few minutes.

Then, as we stopped at a red light, he glanced in my direction. Looking me in the eye, without pausing for a breath, he let loose with a long list of slang terms describing every sexual act imaginable. I was nonplussed, shocked that all those words were common to him. My jaw dropped and my eyes opened like a deer in headlights as I wondered how he had come to hear or know any of those terms. Recognizing my bewilderment, Dad assured me that he knew exactly what all those words meant. As had his father before him, along with his father's father, and so on. In fact, they'd been around a long, long time.

"And chum," he told me, "if you ever want or need to talk to me about anything—anything whatsoever—you can, you know. There's no reason to be concerned or feel embarrassed. I'll never pass judgment. You can ask me or tell me anything you want in confidence, son. I'll always be honest with you."

Dad was true to his word. We'd have wide-ranging discussions, sometimes around the family dinner table or in private when needed. I always felt free to share my perspective, even if it was just my teenage opinion on things, without any sense of disapproval, shame, or judgment.

My parents also had a strong work ethic and were themselves hard working. Dad and Mom always emphasized to us boys the value of a dollar and the importance of earning money. We were taught to establish a savings account for the purpose of contributing to our education or social life whenever possible.

During the tree house years, my brothers and I often did neighborhood odd jobs like mowing lawns, shoveling snow, raking leaves, and even cleaning garages to earn extra money. At one point I had three different paper routes: *The Plain Dealer* at 4:00 a.m. daily with Tim, *The Sun Herald* once a week with my "cousin" Paul, and *The Cleveland Press* solo in the evenings.

The Sunday edition of *The Plain Dealer* mandated a big wagon on which to pull the bulky stacks with their special sections. Tim and I could be seen in the wee hours trudging against a biting wind through two feet of snow.

My first real job came when I was fourteen, washing dishes and bussing tables at the Tokyo Garden restaurant. It was the first of several jobs in the restaurant business. Then there was the summer Tim and I made a small fortune painting house addresses on the curbs in many of the neighborhoods on Cleveland's west side. Following Dad's business advice added to our success. He helped us realize that selling the service to individual homes would be time-consuming and labor-intensive. Plus, limiting the feature to paying clients alone would be aesthetically unappealing for the rest of the street. So, we painted the addresses of every house on a given street. One of us would lay down a white block background next to the driveway apron. The other guy would follow behind, using stencils to paint the house number in black.

When we finished a street, we'd run its length together, crossing the front lawns and wedging flyers with empty "donation" envelopes into doorjambs or mailboxes. The notice informed the homeowner of our names, described our efforts at earning money for college, and requested a donation for the service we had provided. It also instructed the home-owner to leave the donation in the attached envelope sticking out from their screen door after 6:00 p.m.

Then, immediately after dinner, we'd run down every street we had painted that day, collecting the envelopes that were poking from doors like signal flags awaiting our retrieval. The donations were usually more generous than anything we'd have charged.

We had a sweet thing going for some weeks, until we got a visit from the police one evening. They informed us that we didn't have the appropriate business license we needed. This was a setback. We reasoned that we were not selling a service but giving one freely while encouraging support through voluntary donations. Feeling appropriately justified and after some discussion, Tim and I added police lookout to the duties of the guy painting the white block backgrounds. If he spotted official city vehicles or police cars, we'd cut through the yards to a parallel or cross street and continue painting over there.

In due course, though, weary from evading the cops and running out of unpainted curbs, we were forced into retirement. By then school had resumed anyway.

9

BONDS

The first ten days at Metro leading up to my near-death experience had all been a hazy blur of flaming pain. I had no idea regarding the direction or course my life was heading from this point in time. It was all so unbelievable; an unfathomable, unstoppable train had slammed into me and all I knew was that there was a mountain to climb. The major burns I had suffered meant that I was faced with the prospect of being forever different on the outside. *Will that make me different on the inside too? Just who am I?*

Though they were certainly magnified by the undeniable impact of the trauma I had experienced, these were not altogether new questions. Like most teenagers, I'd been making my way and determining my identity for some time. At home and in my parents' circles, my role was to be the model McDonough, the oldest son leading four younger brothers.

I did this by default, drawing from the resources that were the capricious products of an increasingly dysfunctional set of circumstances rather than those of the picture-perfect family we presented. Sure, most of the lessons and skills were learned through the wisdom gleaned from my parents. But many were habitual reactions to the errors in their ways. Regardless, as the glue of home began to weaken and separate, other bonds became more important.

The journey through the middle school years is a trip on which most young people are confronted by a confusing jumble of road signs. Roadblocks. Diversions. Halts. U-turns. And then there are the challenges that come with hormonal surges: sexual maturation completely changes the dynamics in relationships with the opposite sex, further adding to the disarray associated with the first attempts at defining identity.

Naturally, I wanted to fit in with others, to be accepted. At the same time I disliked the idea of cliques and resented the way they often made kids feel that conforming to one standard or another was necessary. I was never quite sure where I would be best received or where I most wanted to be: among the athletic "jocks," the free and independent "beats," or the high-achieving "geeks." There was a bit of each in me.

It mattered not; regardless of individual drifts or directions, looking back it's blatantly obvious that we were all similar in our fears, uncertainties, and insecurities. Another reason I continued to resist the struggle to define my identity through cliques was that it often seemed to involve the juvenile persecution of those who were different.

In my early teens, a number of my close friends were jocks. I wasn't very tall or big, but I was tenacious, played football, swam competitively, and was on the wrestling team. Dad taught my brothers and me to swim almost before we could walk, so I'd grown to love the water and excelled in free-style, breaststroke, and backstroke (butterfly not so much). Wrestling required similar all-around fitness and strength, and I enjoyed my share of triumphs on the junior high team. I even attended an intensive wrestling camp with Tim one summer and was encouraged to pursue the sport more seri-ously, being told I had some real potential, but it demanded more commitment than I was prepared to give. Can't say I was a jock.

Geeks were typically the most academically inclined. They were often found in band, glee club, or theater, clubs that I also enjoyed, as they tapped into my artistic side. Mom always encouraged my singing, perhaps remembering the many hours we had spent singing together in the car as we traveled to and from Rainbow when I'd been sick as a child. She thought I had a great voice and even encouraged me to try out for the prestigious Vienna Boys Choir. I was to attend one of their trials in Cleveland, but then Mom and Dad became busy con-templating a house move (which ended up not happening) and we never followed up on the selection process.

Out of the seventy grade school boys who auditioned for our local high school production of Lionel Bart's musical *Oliver!*, I was one of the seven or eight chosen for roles. I got the part of Charlie Bates and also played one of the orphans, which gave me a taste of theater that I regretfully never pur-sued. But perhaps that decision prevented me from one day having to confront the implications of a disfiguring burn in-jury in an environment so centered on physical appearance.

Despite playing trumpet, some guitar, and piano, singing in glee club, and loving theater, I never pursued any of the arts fully. Nor did I have the necessary affinity for academic diligence, despite having the ability. Can't say I was a geek.

Certainly, on any occasion, it was easy to identify with the beats. In the progressively liberated society of the mid-seventies, many were looking for a party.

Yet while I had alliances with different school groups, my most formative relationships were those in which I shared a connection free from the pressure of cliques. Here I found friends on whom I could rely for support. Many of them lived in or near "the neighborhood," which consisted of three to four blocks at the south end of West 224th Street, where my soon-to-be best friend Tweeter lived, and two cross streets on the southwest border of our suburb, Fairview Park.

Tweeter and I met at school during lunchtime and we quickly became brothers from different mothers. He was charismatic, a larger-than-average guy with an athletic build and confident gait. His light brown hair was parted on the left, like my own, framing ice-blue eyes and chiseled features. His smile was warm and inviting, though his outward demeanor was serious much of the time. He was intelligent, a formidable conversationalist, but when he found a situation humorous nothing could stifle his infectious laugh. Along with his unassuming grin, this laugh was an effective chick magnet, which I quietly envied.

Tweeter was an adroit and capable basketball player, turning out for the school team and keeping himself in good standing with the jocks through his abilities and dedication. He was also sharp at billiards, this being attributable to his superior talents in math and geometry. We had a mutual respect for academic achievement, which we kept discreet, not wanting to appear too bookish to others.

Though I never had Tweeter's aptitude for basketball or pool, we both had a taste for the finer things in life, which we knew required money. He was one of my first buddies to own a car, and from the ninth grade on we always had part-time jobs. Occasionally we worked for the same employer, such as the Brown Derby steakhouse. During one brief period, we attended school from 8:00 a.m. until 3:30 p.m., then carpooled thirty minutes to a grueling job in a plastic factory from 4:00 p.m. until midnight, always trying to save money for college.

With light brown hair and steel-blue eyes, Buddy was a loyal friend who didn't have a mean bone in him. He was always trying to take ownership of my shirts since we were similar in height. Gentle and usually thoughtful of others, he had a generous heart, all of which sometimes made him a pawn of girlfriends. His manner, which caused some people to dismiss him as being slightly slow on the uptake, belied his keener than average insights into the world.

The nickname "Billy Bong" says it all about another noteworthy comrade. Academic achievement was low on his priority list, but a strong work ethic had him holding a part- or full-time job from the age of twelve or thirteen, ensuring that he always had the means to provide the necessary paraphernalia for a party.

There were many other pals worthy of acknowledgment, such as Sean and Dino, two guys who were proud of their respective Irish and Italian cultural roots. Sean had smiling eyes and never missed an opportunity to party. Dino loved cars and motorcycles, and his mannerisms were soft-spoken and reserved.

Another off-and-on best pal was Mark, aka "Piggy." He and I shared many adventures and firsts together, cruising around Cleveland, going to concerts and seeing our favorite bands and singers: Bruce Springsteen, Pink Floyd, and Led Zeppelin to name a few. And we were usually buzzed in the front rows.

Most of my friends and I shared a forever-unslaked thirst for music. I had discovered it in the fourth grade, tuning my transistor radio to CKLW out of Detroit. I soaked up lyrics and styles from Motown R & B to pop, rock, and even some country. I really began to appreciate the art of songwriting and had an affinity for rock and folk. In my journals I was forever writing prose that would form poems or songs. An audiophile before it was a term, I learned to pair any media source with remote speakers hijacked from old appliances. Living in the suburbs of a city that was pretty much the cross-roads of the American concert circuit and the eventual home of the Rock & Roll Hall of Fame, there was no shortage of live music. One of the first shows I attended was an all-day festival at the Cleveland Stadium: Todd Rundgren, Peter Frampton, Uriah Heap, Blue Oyster Cult, and Aerosmith.

Like many kids, I wanted to be in a band. Having learned piano and trumpet, I got an electric guitar while in junior high. Tim played drums and, together or in bands, we performed at a few gigs or school dances. I never expected it to go anywhere, but it was a fun fantasy.

Girls were something of a mystery to me in the early years, having grown up in a majority male household. My first kisses were probably as an innocent second grader with Cathy L. and Mary Rattigan. As my hormones kicked in, girls became more and more central.

10

AFTERMATH

The first days after my near-death experience on the operating table were something of a blur. I drifted between sleepy and groggy, a thickness of clouds and fog dulling my senses. Then there were brief moments of lucidity when I would be consumed by pain. My abdomen felt like an overstuffed suitcase ready to burst open and spew its contents onto my bed.

The burning was intensified with each breath, my lungs slowly filling with secretions. It hurt so much to cough, especially while being intubated. It felt once again like I was choking on a garden hose. But if they removed the breathing tube too soon, I might not be able to maintain adequate oxygen saturations, an indicator that my breaths were not deep enough or were mixed with secretions.

Lying there I still felt powerless in terms of the actual control I had over my surroundings, even though I was awake and not paralyzed. The breathing tube precluded any type of quality communication. I was miserable, smothered in a thick and murky pall of doom. Short of rendering me unconscious, there was little anyone could do to make me more comfortable.

Even worse than the physical sensations or the grief over Mom and Toby was a profound and acute new sense of loss. I yearned to recapture the feeling of security I had sensed as I floated blissfully between that euphoric state in the operating room and some other eternal place beyond the threshold I'd envisioned. I had to keep telling myself that Mom and Toby were okay now, at peace. I still missed them fiercely, but sensing their presence had been so precious.

My anguish was over something that seemed to be tantalizingly beyond my mental and spiritual reach but that I knew was out there—like the dials I couldn't reach on the television in my room. I longed to return to that place of utter peace and contentment I recalled, to the keen sense of truth and awareness of all things. I had never known such an emotional refuge. But it seemed to be evaporating, like a rain cloud or ozone mist that sadly dissipates with the sun's rays after a spring shower. I knew that I'd enjoyed unequivocal safety and contentment, confident of the perfect order to things. Yet, that very real sentiment was slipping from my grasp.

Meanwhile, I began to piece together all that had happened as I cataloged bits of information gathered from the hospital staff and Dad. People kept telling me that I had been fortunate to survive the fire and also to be alive following the surgery. But it certainly became clear to me that fortune had nothing to do with either.

I'd been wheeled into the operating room just before 8:00 a.m. for what should have been a relatively short procedure, the first run at some serious cleansing and debriding of my burns. But it was more than thirteen hours before I emerged, during which time my body had been pushed to its extreme limits.

The debridement had started well. The doctors were using a Watson knife, a sharp steel instrument rather like a giant potato peeler, with a razor slightly longer than a barber's straight blade. The surgeon utilized a back and forth sawing motion to excise the damaged skin and burn wound, collectively referred to as eschar. This resulted in a fair amount of blood loss, which was to be expected.

But then suddenly there was blood everywhere, and not just limited to the areas where they were working; it was draining profusely from my rectum. They had to open me up to find and eradicate the source of the hemorrhage.

Before proceeding, the chief surgeon broke scrub, leaving the OR to go out to the waiting room and speak with my father. He wanted to be certain that Dad understood such an intervention came with high risk, even of death, as my condition was critical.

They began with an exploratory laparotomy, a long vertical incision from sternum to lower abdomen through which they could explore the internal compartments. The procedure confirmed suspicions: the cause of the bleeding was a Curling's stress ulcer.

This was not an uncommon complication among severe burn patients at the time, more frequently occurring after a large quantity of blood loss or other major stressor, as in my case. The body's increased stress leads to excess production of acid in the gut. This is usually an involuntary response that enables the digestion of food to meet increased energy demands in response to trauma. But because of bleeding elsewhere, the usual blood supply to the stomach and duodenum is compromised, a condition known as ischemia. Dr. Thomas Curling first described this process in the 1820s, observing how it causes a violent, bursting sore or ulceration that leads to further bleeding.

These days, readily available acid blockers like Pepcid or Zantac minimize the effects of acid secretion that would otherwise damage normal mucosa. But in 1976 such prophylaxis was not yet understood. Its absence proved nearly fatal in my case.

Having identified the cause of my serious bleeding, the surgical team had to move quickly. They performed a Billroth I procedure, or hemigastrectomy, removing more than half of my damaged stomach and then reconnecting the remaining portion to the small intestine.

All of this was more than enough of an assault on my already weakened body. In fact, one reason that the doctors had waited ten days before considering any surgery was because they knew I wouldn't have been physiologically strong enough to tolerate the stress of the debridement any sooner. It turned out that perhaps I was strong enough to tolerate it—just not while I was awake!

The scouring I'd felt shuddering along my arms and across my abdomen had been the debridement, where the surgeons were excising the deeper burns and damaged tissues with their sharp instruments. That awful slicing sensation I had experienced was the doctors cutting burned tissue from my torso and then opening my abdomen, hoping to save my life.

The burning electric shocks were felt when they used electrocautery to staunch smaller bleeding vessels. I had been awake but unable to move. Feeling these physical assaults pushed my body beyond what may have otherwise been tolerable limits.

The incidence of "unintended intraoperative awareness" has yet to be determined, but it is a recognized potential complication during anesthesia. Putting patients under for surgery often includes the administration of three different drug types: one to inhibit memory, one to decrease pain, and one to inhibit movement in select cases.

If patients have been paralyzed by drugs but are not receiving enough analgesic to mask the pain, they may be conscious, aware of all that is happening but simply unable to communicate that they're awake. When they are fully paralyzed, patients are not capable of blinking or opening their eyes, twitching a finger, or breathing. Without artificial or mechanical ventilation, the patient will die.

The terror of complete powerlessness while conscious is beyond description. These days anesthesiologists are able to prevent this complication by utilizing special brain wave activity monitors that alert them to a patient's conscious or awake state. But not then: I was mentally awake, fully conscious, feeling every stab and slash of pain but unable to raise an alarm or communicate a distress signal in any fashion.

Such an experience can linger emotionally with a patient long after the actual event, producing a kind of PTSD. But more immediately, it can push already life-threatening procedures to the brink, destabilizing vital signs. In my case, the trauma provoked a massive adrenaline surge, increasing my heart rate while further increasing the acidity of the stomach lining.

The body can only take so much: the ulceration of my stomach lining along with blood loss caused my heart to stop. I was as good as dead. What should have been a serious, delicate, but still fairly predictable procedure suddenly became a life-or-death emergency. The surgical team went into a full-court press.

The first I knew of everything that had happened was when I came to, back in the BICU, shortly after 11:00 p.m. Still groggy, I could first hear and then see Dad sitting at my bedside as I began opening my eyes intermittently. The details I understood were sketchy, but there was a new source of pain, tightness, and cramping in my lower abdomen. Looking down, I could see where a large incision had been made in my distended and swollen belly, which was now partially closed with long wire bands called temporary retention sutures.

As the nurses scurried in and out of the room tending to various tasks and my postoperative care, each one commented on my brush with death.

"Young man, you nearly bought the farm today," one said.

"It was really touch and go there for a while," said another.

As I lay there trying to make sense of the drama and the nurses' depictions of my close call, ironically my first thought was not about the severity of my burns but rather, *I wonder if that's going to leave a big scar on my stomach.* At the same time, I seemed fully aware of the day's events, certainly of surviving the near fatality. Everything Dad described felt like déjà vu, as though he were simply reminding me of what I already knew about the all-day marathon in the OR.

One constant through all those early days was my father. All of the frustrations or arguments we'd ever had were forgotten. My occasional teenage rebellion didn't matter. It seemed he was always there at the hospital, encouraging me and convincing me that things were going to work out.

Since the morning after his flight back from San Francisco, Dad had been spending the majority of his time at my bedside or in the waiting room of the burn unit. He was barely getting the minimum hours of necessary sleep and was surviving on hospital vending machine food—primarily Campbell's soup and Lance peanut butter crackers.

He made every effort to be strong and brave for all of us, but sometimes the mask would slip and I could see the hurt and sadness or loneliness in his eyes. My heart went out to him in his grief, and I wondered how he was managing to hold up under all of the strain. *No heart is ever made to stand or survive such breakage*, I thought.

One night, before the first surgery, Dad was sitting at my bedside as usual at the end of another long and trying day. As we waited together for the doctors to make their evening rounds, his face looked drawn and sallow. His eyelids were heavy as he fought against fatigue, slumped down in the orange vinyl chair. Somehow he had managed to keep up appearances, though, wearing dress slacks and a white oxford shirt with the sleeves rolled up to mid-forearm. His perfectly knotted and dimpled tie was loosened around the neck. His head was gently nodding to the side when suddenly he jerked up, alert and awake.

"I can't believe it!" he shouted, eyes wide. "I haven't even asked Packy how his arm feels!"

Packy had landed heavily after leaping to safety from his bedroom window. He seemed to be okay though, and the fall was forgotten in all the ensuing confusion and chaos. It wasn't until a couple of days later, while staying with the Rattigans, that Packy complained of lingering pain. A trip to the ER and an X-ray revealed that he had fractured his left radius.

Dad was wracked with remorse for not remembering to check with Packy to see how he was doing. His ten-year-old son had lost his mother and a brother, narrowly escaped with his life, and had his left arm in a cast and sling, and yet he'd somehow been overlooked. Dad's shoulders seemed to sag for a moment as he was overcome with the magnitude of everything he was carrying. He took a handkerchief from his pocket, blew his nose, and shuddered with sighs, surrendering with exasperation as he wiped the tears from his eyes.

For my part, I was grateful for his presence and concern, but also felt somewhat guilty that I was the center of his attention when there were so many other things demanding his time, including my brothers, whom I desperately wanted to see. I wanted to hold them all close, as if somehow together we could dampen the pain we all were feeling.

Until my medical status progressed from "critical" to "guarded," my visitors were limited to immediate family but excluded anyone under sixteen years of age. So I had yet to see Tim, Dan, or Packy. Dad updated them daily on my condition, but they were anxious to see me face-to-face. I was equally eager to see them, to hug them and remind them how much they were loved. Just thinking of their narrow escape from the fire consistently brought tears to my eyes.

Lying there thinking of them, there was no doubt in my mind that our mutual suffering and the loss of Mom and Toby would bond us together with unconditional love beyond that of ordinary brothers. Through this struggle, I instantly knew I would always love my brothers, immensely more deeply and differently than I would have otherwise.

The hospital's rigid restrictions were relaxed as doctors recognized greater benefit than risk in allowing Tim and Dan to visit me. They arrived in the burn unit together but were quiet and reserved upon seeing me covered in bandages and surrounded by all of the medical paraphernalia. The setting alone would have been overwhelming for ten-year-old Packy, so his visits were deferred until later. But after another couple of weeks he too was permitted to visit, at which time it was readily apparent that his bravery and courage were on equal par with his older brothers.

On their first visits Tim and Dan were required to don the standard paper wardrobe, including masks, hats, and gowns, which they wore over their Army-Navy policeman's jackets, Levi's jeans, and Frye boots. They were of similar stature, with hair parted in the middle and nearly to shoulder length.

Their lower faces were hidden behind paper surgical masks that failed to hide their pain; I could see it in their teary, glassy eyes that held residual innocence, some remaining evidence of our mother's love, which had nurtured them to the verge of manhood. At the same time, their tears seemed to hint at emotional scar tissue beginning to form as a wall of protection against the world.

Their youthful faces appeared slightly intimidated at seeing me so helpless. Yet each immediately gave me a gentle hug, though I'm sure there was some hesitation for fear of hurting me. I hadn't realized how much I missed and needed their company and their hugs.

The outpouring of love and condolences from our entire community was remarkable. News of the fire and the tragic loss suffered by our family dominated the local media for several weeks. Both Mom and Dad were loved and known all over town, which was reflected in the far-reaching support and gestures of kindness. At the funerals for Mom and Toby, I was told, the procession of cars extended for miles.

Mayor Perk sent me a personal letter expressing his sympathy for what I had experienced, and an official city proclamation citing my bravery and courage, saying that I had been a hero in rescuing my brothers from the fire. I was humbled by the gesture but found it hard to really accept his words. I felt more guilt and the shame of failure, nothing like a hero.

In addition to having plenty of visitors, including celebrities from the Cleveland Browns, Cavaliers, and Indians, I was getting inundated with mail. Boxes full of cards and letters were delivered daily to my bedside, expressing love and care from relatives, friends, and even strangers all over the country. The mail quickly began to pile up and had to be sent home with Dad, along with a canoe paddle wood-burned by the Quinn family and other friends who spent summers with us at the lake.

The Quinns, along with my friend Jeff's family, spent many vacations with us in Huron, Ohio. Jeff, my brothers, and I would use Grandpa's aluminum boat to explore the best of Lake Erie's shoreline while fishing for tasty perch and bass. We would clean our fish at dusk on a cliff overlooking the water, later sleeping under the stars.

Some of my most loyal and devoted supporters were my high school friends: Buddy, Billy, and Dino, among others. Topping the list though was Tweeter, who came second only to Dad in the level of devotion and commitment he displayed. From the first time that I was allowed to receive visitors, Tweeter came virtually every day until I was discharged months later. This was no small commitment; he'd often round up two or three others to come along with him, all of whom were motivated to cheer me up.

Tweeter's steadfastness was even more remarkable considering that my attitude often failed to reflect my gratitude. I was glad for his care and company, but some days the pain and my seemingly glacial progress would leave me in a dark mood so that I didn't really want to socialize. Tweeter took it all in stride, sitting quietly in the chair next to me until it was time to go.

Sometimes it might have felt like it, but I was not alone.

11

PROGRESS

Mountaintop encounters such as a near-death experience affect people in different ways. Some seem compelled to shout about it from the rooftops, sharing the event with as many as possible, while for others it is almost too intimate to readily reveal. Although initially I didn't fully comprehend all that had happened, I knew that I was profoundly, forever changed.

On a positive note, I knew God was with me. He had become a new and very real presence in my life. But from a medical perspective, things were not so optimistic. Post-operatively, my status remained critical for weeks. For the doctors there was a low threshold for returning me to the operating room at the first sign of any further trouble.

My potential for taking a turn for the worse was high. Because of the large volume of blood loss, cardiac arrhythmias, and my prolonged time under general anesthesia, I was at risk for a variety of complications. Prolonged anesthesia time increases the risk for developing pneumonia. Indeed, my temperature was moderately elevated for quite a few days following surgery, which doctors attributed to consolidation of lower lung secretions and the large volume of blood transfusions—I had required more than thirty units that day alone. Also, I'd had multiple episodes of chills that no quantity of warm blankets seemed to alleviate.

Finally, after what seemed like a lifetime, my respiratory status stabilized enough that the doctors were able to extubate me. I was breathing on my own again through a green plastic oxygen mask. Still to this day the smell of those green masks or their silicone tubing brings me right back to the burn unit and my hospital room: the odors, the dark tile floors, and the paste-colored walls. Between therapeutic breathing treatments, I occasionally tried to talk but was only able to generate a raspy whisper. The first night off the ventilator, I murmured to Dad, "Do you really believe in God and that Mom and Toby are in heaven?"

Without hesitation he replied, "You bet, chum."

I responded saying that I knew it to be true, that I had been with them and Jesus on the evening of my surgery. I attempted to describe the loving and beautiful feeling, so hard to put into words adequately but also so very real and certain.

Dad seemed genuinely excited by my account. Then he recounted the circumstances surrounding the events of that Friday the thirteenth and how it was such a close call.

"I couldn't bear the thought of losing you," he said. "I told the doctors to do everything necessary to keep you alive. And I prayed that God would give you the fortitude and grace to survive."

I was amazed to hear this, touched to think that he had been praying even as I was in God's presence. This shared experience seemed to draw us even closer together, rekindling and forging a bond through mutual fear, grief, loss, and profound pain.

Any vague suspicion I may have had that Dad was accepting of my near-death account simply out of empathy was dismissed once and for all by someone else's keen interest in what I had to say: Dr. Frat.

The director of the burn unit, Dr. Richard B. Fratianne, had been out of town on the night of my admission. We had heard about the renowned leader of the medical team caring for me but had not met him until a few days after the surgery, as the haze lifted and I began to recover.

Dr. Frat—the diminutive used by veterans of the unit staff—was the founder of the burn unit and considered one of the world's leading experts in all aspects of burn care. Having initially trained as a general and trauma surgeon, he had devoted his career to the specialty.

Before meeting him, we had learned that he was a man of faith who attended Mass every Sunday, often in the hospital chapel; it seemed he was always on duty. He was also known to be fond of his curved-stem pipe, like that of Sherlock Holmes, which he occasionally even smoked on rounds.

Dad was in his usual bedside chair during visiting hours the evening we met Dr. Frat. We could see out into the ward from my room in the critical section of the West Tower circle, where automatic double doors provided access to the unit for professionals and staff only. From that same window overlooking the nurses' station we could see that evening medical rounds were beginning as evidenced by the congregation of bodies in white coats and scrubs. Clinical professors, attending doctors, medical residents, an intern, medical students, nurses, PTs, OTs, RTs, and dietitians, among others, were all convened outside the first patient's room.

There was obviously teaching underway as the mob progressed slowly around the circle. As the group approached my room, we heard intermittent voices speaking in the foreign tongues of med-speak, as well as an occasional hearty kind of deep laugh.

Dr. Frat wore wire-rimmed glasses and had crystal clear, penetrating eyes set in a chiseled face accented by a warm smile. He introduced himself and the medical team before beginning a discourse on my history and condition, including the close call with death. His serene nature and confidence immediately won Dad over and left us both feeling that somehow everything was going to be okay.

Having completed the visit, Dr. Frat assured us that we'd be talking later in greater detail. Then the team followed him from the room while feverishly jotting down orders and crossing things off their lists.

One Sunday morning after Mass in the hospital chapel, I recounted my near-death experience to Dr. Frat. I knew he believed in God but was uncertain how he'd receive my account. He showed genuine interest as I spoke, although his first concern was that I'd been awake during the surgery. He asked me more about what had happened so that he could discuss the incident with the anesthesiologist. Sometime later he came to me to ask for more details about what I remembered.

"You're not alone, Mark," he told me, after listening thoughtfully to what I said. "I have heard of other patients who have had near-death experiences similar to yours."

It was the first time I had heard that term used to describe what I had gone through, and it would not be the last time he and I would discuss the events of that day. He validated my belief that a spiritual experience had indeed taken place. I was left with the impression that sometimes things happen that science alone cannot explain.

Once it was clear that I was beginning to mend from the latest surgery, Dr. Frat and his team began to establish a game plan for managing the obstacles ahead. They were careful not to overwhelm me by explaining how far away the destination lay, but how by achieving short-term goals an end point was within reach.

They wanted to continue with more debridement of the burns they'd begun working on when their efforts were cut short during the last surgery. They were going to begin transfusing blood plasma preoperatively, in anticipation of more blood loss. There would be many surgeries before my ultimate discharge, and each would likely include one of the multiple forms of skin grafting, named by their source, thickness, and preparation.

Once again I was yearning for oral hydration, having been NPO since the evening before surgery—and now post-operatively for five days or more to ensure that normal bowel function would resume. The first sign that everything was okay would be a quiet rumbling of my stomach, along with flatulence. Somewhere around a week post-op, my wish for progress was granted, and I was finally able to offer irre-futable evidence of intestinal integrity, without evidence of leakage.

Shortly after this usually less-celebrated bodily function had been documented by one of the nurses, the resident intern came into my room. "Well, I'm guessing it won't be long till you're asking for the bedpan!" he declared as though I had realized some kind of major achievement. He wrote orders for me to resume my diet with clear then full liquids.

I had to wait another whole day before I was granted my favorite comfort food: toast with butter, made fresh in the unit kitchen by Roberta, one of the nurses' aides, who could always cheer me up on a gloomy day. My mood lightened, although it was short-lived as I began to wonder, *Will I ever be lovable with scars over much of my body?*

Regretfully, my first bites of food were not nearly as euphoric as my first sips of water had been. Everything I put in my mouth seemed to have the same bland taste. The resident intern seemed disappointed when I failed to display the gleeful expression he had anticipated.

Regardless of the number of surgeries I'd require, my body needed optimal fuel sources to accommodate the healing process. Ideally, the extra calories I needed—rather like a high-performing athlete, even though I was in a hospital bed—would normally be absorbed through an increased daily diet. Unfortunately, the surgical procedure that saved my life had necessitated the removal of more than half of my stomach.

Although the rejoined parts of my intestines were functioning, the relative amounts of food I could consume and store were significantly reduced. In the meantime, the ratio of calories consumed to those burned would be notably less than optimal. The doctors said my stomach would stretch to normal over time, but that didn't help matters now.

Other factors contributing to my puny appetite included intermittent acute depression. Despite trying to hold near to my heart the transcendent moments I had experienced, it felt like they were close to being pulled from my grip. And then there were likely many side effects of the pharmacopeia of medicines flowing through my system. Rather quickly I lost over twenty-five pounds, and dietitians anticipated I'd lose more than twice that amount before discharge, even with intervention.

So, my best efforts at the prescribed feeding regimen, including smaller amounts with increased frequency, were augmented with a nasogastric feeding tube, which was unpleasant in its own way. The tube passed through the nose and directly into my esophagus, allowing liquid calories to be infused directly into my stomach.

Having gone for so long without eating interfered with my taste buds, one of the residents told me, but with time my appetite would improve. The opportunity to test this theory was brief, however. I was told that I would be returning to surgery early on the morning after next and would therefore again be NPO at midnight the following day.

12

DYSFUNCTION

Much of my idle time in the hospital was focused on getting back to normal, but deep down I had no clue what "normal" meant, let alone how to return to it. Home was a blackened shell, and wherever Dad, my brothers, and I finally landed, there would always be two big voids left by the absence of Mom and Toby.

Even without those losses, the reality was that things had been quietly unraveling at home for some time before the flames. Those glancing at the McDonough family from the outside probably saw the quintessential all-American family, a picture-perfect scene. But closer inspection would have revealed some blemishes in the portrait, a few tight smiles hiding private concerns.

As with most children, our understanding of life was a mixture of lessons "taught and caught," meaning the values and principles clearly described and demonstrated as well as those we picked up indirectly by what we observed and experienced.

For the most part, my parents and most all of their acquaintances were excellent role models. That is to say they had no outwardly blatant character defects or bad habits. As I grew to be older and wiser, though, I allowed most of those adult role models to come down from the pedestals on which I'd naively placed them.

Like most prosperous folks in those days, my parents liked to celebrate and share their success with family and friends. As proud Irish descendants, they once hosted an epic St. Patrick's Day party where Tim and I dressed as leprechauns and greeted guests alongside our Peekapoo dog that had been dyed green. Young as we were, we were ripe to surreptitiously sample the green beer and other drinks as we carried glasses into the kitchen.

Needless to say, smoking, drinking, and partying were normal pastimes in those days, particularly among the adults and parents of our generation. In retrospect, such habits were less than ideal for role models, but they were the societal norm. Ironically, they were even seen as markers for maturity, success, and being "all grown up." Unfortunately, such antics were occasionally taken to excess and began to introduce harmful dysfunctional behavior into some relationships, especially within the family, though it would be some time before the effects became evident.

Gradually, subtly, things began to change. The shine dimmed. As a prominent corporate investment counselor, it was not uncommon for Dad to find himself at a martini sales lunch. Partying on weekends gradually evolved to regular happy hours during the week—a Scotch or two before dinner, more of the same after dessert. With the stressors of afflu-ence, what had always just seemed a norm started to become something of a need.

I knew that Dad's father had been an alcoholic, but it was never really discussed openly. Dad did speak about how his father, a type A personality, was frequently unavailable to his children in the evenings. Dad vowed that such a scenario would not be repeated in his own life.

It was easier to stay in denial than to confront my par-ents' drinking problem directly. Regardless, I could not deny the symptoms, and I learned to have my antennae up in the evenings so that I could read the signals. After a drink or two, Mom would more often than not become talkative and gregarious. But eventually her overly affec-tionate silliness grew old, even offensively aggravating. Other times she could be capricious, vacillating between attentively curious and carelessly indifferent. That could be entertaining, if a little undependable, and it wasn't long before we learned that evenings were not the most reliable hours for serious discussions. I don't know that Mom had a drinking problem, at least not one of her own admis-sion. It was more that sometimes her drinking contrib-uted additional problems. Some experts would label it a codependency.

Following happy hour, it was not uncommon for Mom to have a sudden change of mind or mood over anything, subtly infusing us with a feeble sense of security. Sometimes I'd swing between feeling guilty for arguing disrespectfully with her and resentful of her unpredictable mood changes. Either one of us could become petulant or passive-aggressive if the other disagreed. Subsequently, avoidance by one or both would follow, snowballing the overall effect and further obfuscating anything close to direct communication.

For his part, Dad could also be fickle, fluctuating between being apathetic and demanding. He often had high expectations of himself, which he would then impose on his sons. This was not too bad when he was sober, but after a few drinks he could become quite intimidating; he was a master at suddenly making his disapproval obvious, prompting any of us to become combative. This made the issue about *our* behavior instead of his as the one instigating the conflict. It was rare to see my parents awkwardly drunk, nor were they ever violent. But as the evenings wore on, often they would become increasingly distant, unavailable, or at least unreliable. In our case, we learned to chart our own courses as Mom and Dad learned to let go. However, the dysfunction of alcoholism disrupts otherwise normal dynamics, not to mention provoking anger, hurt feelings, and raised voices through unhealthy conflict resolution.

While the growing uncertainty in our home was frustrating, even more difficult was the sense of loss I felt but could not clearly identify or express. The portrait of the idyllic parents I'd adoringly carried since my youth had begun to fade like a photograph left out in the sun. Most frustrating was that the emotional attachment I felt conflicted with the intellectual detachment I displayed, further aggravating the situation. And in addition to my own mixture of confused feelings, I felt a responsibility as the oldest son to protect the younger ones from the resulting turmoil.

A general air of truculence wafted through the house, with all parties ready to take a stand, stubbornly defensive or obstinate. Many times I went to bed feeling unheard by my parents, despite my best efforts to communicate my needs or wants. Imprinted deeply within was the message "Your needs are unimportant." I didn't realize it at the time, but as we became increasingly antagonistic, we were all exhibiting some of the classic signs of alcoholic dysfunction.

A family functions like a complex machine, with numerous gears and wheels moving together and dependent upon one another. When one part of the machine malfunctions, eventually it breaks down and becomes dysfunctional as the other parts try to adapt or accommodate to the changing system. Ironically, the roles to which individuals within a system adapt allow the family to seem more functional than it really is. Various identities arise in an effort to maintain a normal appearance according to society's expectations.

Family therapists and counselors have described specific roles that characterize family members affected by alcoholism or addiction, and we fell into them without realizing it. Along with Dan, I became what experts identify as the "hero child." Often the firstborn or oldest, they are usually seen as a positive, contributing member of the family. Typically overachievers, they try to do the right thing at all times, thereby pleasing Mom and Dad and diverting attention away from the real problem. They're readily identified as leaders, conforming to the expectations of authority figures, but they also like to control the outcome of events and others' behavior, leading to a tendency to be well organized.

Tim frequently fulfilled the role of jester or mascot, striving to maintain harmony at all costs and once again diverting attention from the core issue. Those in this position avoid confrontation by using humor, sarcasm, and quick wit to maintain a lighthearted atmosphere. With a hearty laugh, Tim could find humor in anything, often using impersonations and strange noises to get a laugh. He had any number of routines into which he could roll when there was tension in the room or seriousness on the horizon. Saddled as he was with being the laughter-maker, it was difficult to get him to discuss issues of the heart, though it was always clear there were deep feelings within.

Packy, the number four son, was best characterized as a "lost child" or scapegoat. This role usually includes family members on whom blame is placed for just about anything. As a result, they are most likely to isolate during times of discord, often stomping off to their room to establish physical and emotional walls of avoidance. Denying tension existed, Packy would withdraw from confrontation of any kind—thereby failing to get his needs met while attracting negative attention.

Only six at the time of the fire, Thomas Christopher completed the McDonough clan when he was born on January 20, 1970. Toby, as we all knew him, had an old soul and wisdom beyond his years. Always jovial and gregarious, he was usually able to get his needs satisfied with minimal effort. But if for any reason they were not met, he'd fulfill them himself. Failing this, he could become sullen and emotionally removed. He was a hero child in the making, with some traits typical of a lost child.

Despite the growing divisions, there was still a strong sense of family bond and an unspoken agreement that if we could all just accommodate or somehow maintain a sense of normalcy, everything might yet be okay and the storm looming on the horizon might be stilled.

The kinds of problems we were all having were never addressed directly, so I don't know the reason for sure, but I suspect Dad and Mom suggested a special family road trip the summer after I turned sixteen to in some way recapture the magic of our earlier years.

So my parents revealed their plans: an ambitious two-week vacation that would overshadow all of our previous adventures. We would rent an RV and hit the road to Florida. Destination: Walt Disney World! Along the way we would visit their alma mater, Miami University of Ohio, stop in the Blue Ridge Mountains, and revisit Panama City and the Florida Panhandle, where we had vacationed during our first decade as a family—a reconnection of the McDonoughs. We would even venture as far as Key West before heading to Orlando.

With a fair amount of road time under my belt, I passed my driving test easily when Mom took me to the Bureau of Motor Vehicles the day school let out for the summer. Given that this was only a few weeks before we were due to hit the road, I was aware of the honor and trust Dad was extending by inviting me to assist with the driving. Excitement and anticipation overshadowed the usual tension as we began to plan and map out our journey. This new level of accord was pretty fragile, though, and the cracks were not long in appearing, the result of overambitious and mismatched expectations.

Dad's plan included sharing the wheel and decamping during the wee hours of the morning while the rest of the family slept. We'd be well en route to the next destination before they even woke up.

Mom, meanwhile, had other fantasies altogether that did not include a perpetual state of being on the go. When she woke up the morning after our first overnight halt to find we were already rolling down the road to the next KOA (Kampgrounds of America), a verbal blowout ensued. It did not bode well for the rest of the trip.

Adding turmoil to the mix was our failure to appreciate the time needed for camping and decamping at RV sites. The never-ending stop-and-go demands of daily location changes were physically exhausting. The additional work and preparation quickly grew old and tiresome. Being constantly on the move, with repeated departures from campgrounds in mid or late morning, left few moments for relaxation.

Neither Dad nor any of us boys gave much thought to Mom's perspective, the lone female trapped in a rolling aluminum can with six hyperactive males. She and Dad were soon bickering or exercising their control in small but cumulative squabbles.

Yet there were flickers of what used to be, like the sunlight that would splash through the trees, casting shadows of times past onto the larger-than-life dashboard of our rolling home as we drove along. One such moment came in Panama City Beach as we sauntered along the Gulf shore. We passed a large group of college students as we walked along the sand; they were roasting a pig over a large barbecue pit and whetting their appetites with a keg of beer. By the time the meat was done, so were they: the combination of booze and blazing sun left them too inebriated to know what to do with the tantalizing pork.

As usual, Dad saw a teaching moment not to be wasted. He stepped in to explain—and demonstrate—how to carve the pig. The students thought that he was just the coolest guy around, exclaiming, "Far out, dude. This is excellent!" Party music bubbled through the rich aroma wafting up and down the beach as the sun began to sneak slowly below the western horizon of the Gulf of Mexico. Its rays refracted through the water, casting a warm vermilion glow that blanketed the tropical setting. Sea oats gently swayed in the salty breeze.

As I looked around at the whimsical scene, my father in the middle of it all, my heart swelled with unexpected pride. The emotional vulnerability and euphoria that enveloped me caught me by surprise, familiar from so many years prior. It was a genuine contentment I hadn't known I missed so much until that moment.

O n another evening, having showered the salt from our suntanned bodies, we took a family stroll down the strip. Mom and Dad ambled ahead, hand in hand like newlywed lovebirds. They looked so suave, a handsome couple in love, turning heads as people glanced at them and their brood. I was quietly filled with pride, a thirst I hadn't known existed now smoothly satiated.

If my parents and I had been finding it increasingly difficult to talk directly to each other in meaningful ways, I warmed to what I overheard as they spoke about me while we drove. Bronzed from the sun, shirtless in my usual minimalist wardrobe of cutoff jeans, flip-flops, and Ray-Ban aviator shades, I was concentrating on steering the motor home along one of the endless southern highways as Mom and Dad chatted together. They remarked on how well I handled the vehicle, which made me feel good.

Then Mom added, "He's so darn handsome too. He's likely to break some hearts." This was thrilling and surprising. I almost wanted to ask her to repeat the prodigious remark, but I didn't want her to know I had been listening. I had never considered—or more likely had lost sight of—the positive light in which my parents saw me and my brothers.

Up until then I had not thought of myself as good-looking. I'd not had any difficulty attracting the attention or affections of some of the prettiest girls around, but I'd never stopped to think that others might describe me as attractive. I knew that Dad was striking and hoped that I might have inherited some of his genes, but I was a typical teenage boy, rather insecure about my looks and likability. This snatch of conversation offered some welcome affirmation on our three-thousand-mile trek.

There were also more occasions that provided opportunities for me to flex my independence. I was like Dad in many ways, so having two alpha males sharing the driving duties, each certain that his was the only and best way to get anywhere or do anything, ensured a clash of testosterone.

This was exacerbated by vacation mode, which meant that happy hour for the adults often began at noon. There was usually a cold beer with or for lunch; I'd sometimes get one as well, having been allowed to join them in the occasional drink at home since turning sixteen.

As usual, the moment alcohol was added to the mix, moods and temperaments became unpredictable and fragile. It also meant that the bulk of the driving fell to me—when I didn't have to seize the responsibility for myself. After lunch I'd frequently need to distract Dad by some clever means to keep him from reflexively assuming the driver's seat. Other times I was less tactful in my approach and we ended up just shy of a physical altercation. I'd argue his less than fit state to be at the wheel, forgetting how it might sound coming from a kid who, despite more than a year of driving experience, had only possessed an unrestricted license for two months.

I could probably have been more tolerant many times, but pride in my newly acquired driver's license and frustration with my parents' ways made me stubbornly maintain a righteous sense of responsibility that would not allow me to compromise family safety. Not that I really had any business being self-righteous: on several occasions Dad offered me a beer while I was driving, and I accepted.

Looking back, this gesture of his was probably an effort to alleviate his guilt and justify his own actions. Mom and Dad sometimes squabbled over the small things, but neither was tolerant of the other's drinking. Their fighting spirit spilled over into the rest of the RV, and we boys often ended up antagonizing one another.

Things came to a head as we reached what was supposed to be the high point of the vacation. We'd made it to Walt Disney World in Orlando. My brothers and I had had long talks about the parts of the park we were most looking forward to exploring.

I don't remember the specifics. Maybe Dad had too much of a buzz. Perhaps we were all just tired after another long day on the road. It could have been a simple misunderstanding. The fact that I can't recall the details suggests it was something minor, but it all blew up. Dad was arguing with Mom again, and I was confronting him about something. There were raised voices and lowered tolerance.

Before long the altercation had spilled out of the motor home into the parking lot. Anyone watching must have wondered what we were all doing, fighting at "the happiest place on earth." Then Dad reared back in classic parental posture and barked, "We'll just pull this thing out of here and head home! We're not going into the park. There's no reason to waste any more money on admission to Disney World!" We were all stunned. We knew Dad well enough to understand that this was no empty threat.

The silence that followed was broken by Toby. "Now look what you've done, Mark," he wailed. "We don't get to see Mickey Mouse and Pluto!"

My hot anger cooled in the face of his plaintive cry. I felt awful, like it was entirely my fault that things had deteriorated this way. Whatever the rights or wrongs of the clash with my father, I was determined that my innocent baby brother and the others would not miss out on their first visit to Walt Disney World.

Swallowing my pride, I managed somehow to talk Dad down. He relented, and we went on to explore the parks, putting on our best McDonough faces for the entire world to see. Despite all the tensions and verbal fisticuffs, we returned home in relatively good spirits. There had been flashes of the old family—love, forgiveness, unity, and great fun. Maybe things could yet turn around.

The illusion that we could just go back to the way things were was shattered when we got back to Fairview Park. Our North Park Drive home, the scene of so many happy times, no longer looked the way it had. We had been burgled.

As we walked in, it looked as though some wild force of nature had blown through the property in our absence. Every room had been ransacked and turned inside out. The contents of drawers, cupboards, and cabinets were scattered about the rooms with thoughtless abandon.

Anything of significant value was gone. Among the items stolen were the dining room silver and silverware, jewelry from my parents' room, my Fender guitar and amplifier, and stereo equipment from my room and the main family room. It seemed that the perpetrators had not been worried about being discovered, as they apparently had taken time to consume some of the contents of the liquor cabinet, as evidenced by the empty bottles. Many of the bottles that had been full were missing altogether.

At least one of the culprits had sustained some kind of injury, prompting them to smear the bloody evidence on the walls. Trash and cigarette butts were strewn about several rooms, which combined with the contents of the empty drawers gave the appearance of a chaotic party and its aftermath.

The shock was huge, hitting us broadside as we arrived home weary and ready for familiar comforts. It felt like we had been personally assaulted, as if the intimate nature of family that we had been trying to restore on our trip had been viciously violated. The optimism we'd carried home seemed to evaporate, but not before infusing us with memories of some priceless moments and a sense of unity that we tried to retain.

Picking up the pieces was a frustrating process, especially for Mom. Contacting the insurance company, she was told that she would have to live with the damage until they could schedule an adjuster to evaluate the details on-site.

So it was that the blood smears in the dining room were still visible a week later when I came home, entering through the garage just before midnight on August 2, 1976. The marks were also on the backsplash of the sideboard countertop, where six smoke detectors sat with their backs removed, revealing empty battery compartments.

Dad had left them there after his failed attempt to install them the previous day. They required specific battery types not readily available, so the chore was postponed.

It was to be completed upon his return from San Francisco.

13

SWIMMING

My memory of exactly what happened during those minutes caught in the furnace that was my home remained hazy. Dr. Frat suspected that while attempting to escape from the fire, I had instinctively protected my eyes and face, ducking down as low as possible, unwittingly trading function for appearance. This caused me to sustain relatively superficial burns to my face and neck, with deeper ones to my upper extremities and trunk.

The more minor burns were beginning to heal. The others would require multiple surgeries over time and were at significant risk for contractures, the result of tightening in scar tissue that can severely limit mobility, necessitating further reconstructive surgery.

The injuries to my arms, forearms, and hands, along with parts of my legs, ankles, and feet, were the most violent aspect of the thermal damage. These were the deepest or "full thickness" burns, comprising almost a third of my body surface. "Partial thickness" and "deep partial thickness" burns accounted for the rest.

Paradoxically, more serious and deeper burns are initially less sensitive as their damage extends below the nerve endings. However, once grafting with temporary or permanent skin begins, nerve regeneration soon follows, and with it the return of pain and sensation. More superficial first- and second-degree burns are relatively much more painful to begin with, as damage has occurred to and around the freely exposed nerve endings.

Regardless of my less-than-optimal nutritional status, I survived the next surgeries without complications. The first procedure included more debridement of nonviable tissues and temporary pigskin grafting to my arms. The next surgery involved closing the dorsal surface of my hands.

While being vital to life, water had also always been a key element of my happiness and well-being. At early ages, even before we exhibited the unstable wobbling gait characteristic of toddlers, Dad had taught us boys to swim. We all loved it. Basic aquatic survival skills, including the all-important back float and the basic dog paddle, were among our skill sets as infants. Later, when referencing any body of water, we'd each ask, "Is that over my head?" And Dad would reply, "Even if it is, you know how to swim!"

Clearly taking advantage of my love for water, Dr. Frat and the staff were eager to inform me about an aspect of burn care I'd yet to experience. They explained that during the first week in the unit, my critical condition and dependence on the ventilator had precluded me from experiencing the benefits of whirlpool therapy. However, they explained, "You love to swim, and this therapy is just like swimming!"

The next morning, one of the burn technicians and Carol, my nurse, transferred me from the bed to a gurney. On it was something like a travois, except that instead of two poles with a sling between them, it consisted of a rectangular frame with a vinyl sling tethered to its borders and covered in a clear plastic bag. My body was positioned supine on the stretcher; its edge was digging into the burns of my back. About that time it all went wrong. The wind was knocked from my sails as the tiller flew free from the rudder.

Carol was one of my primary nurses specializing in critical burn care. On first appearance she reminded me of Sister Bertrille, "The Flying Nun" played by Sally Field in the 1960s television series. She was petite, cute, and vivacious, with a gentle demeanor and a magnetic sparkle in her bright smiling eyes. Her soft appearance did not belie her passionate and demanding take-charge nature that befitted her true taskmaster character. Carol's crystal-blue eyes could convince anyone of her point of view, and she insisted upon obedience from me.

She and the tech wheeled me into the large, cold treatment room that had as its centerpiece a massive Hubbard tank, named after the engineer who designed it in the 1920s. With a capacity of 425 gallons, the tank is shaped like a clover. Its narrow middle allows therapists to reach their patient, while the wider ends permit a patient to move their upper and lower extremities. That way PTs and OTs can perform range-of-motion exercises with patients and document more accurate range of motion unencumbered by bulky dressings.

In addition to the seemingly frigid temperature of the room, my body was flushed with chilling waves. This caused me to constrict my arms tightly to my sides, as I could not bend my elbows to hug my chest due to the tightening of grafts and associated loss of elbow flexion.

Carol said that my chills were likely related to an elevated temperature and that the doctors wanted to take down the dressings of my upper extremities so that they could more closely examine the status of the newly placed porcine (pigskin) grafts and rule out infection.

Immediately I was resistant, having been under the impression that post-op dressings need not be changed for five days or longer. Carol explained that my understanding was generally correct, but only if there was no reason to change the dressings sooner. Unfortunately, there was a reason.

Unwrapping and redressing the wounds and all my extremities was a three-hour physical and emotional trauma, exhausting when combined with the unexpected alien appearance of the porcine grafts. They looked like fish scales or alligator skin from being meshed, a process that expands their size by running them through a machine that punches them with a pattern of holes like fishnet stockings.

Despite what I'd been led to expect, a long and winding road lay before me as I dried out from my first "swim" in the hydrotherapy tank. It had been no relaxing day at the pool.

To make matters worse, I learned that my day was not over. Though the doctors had been pleased with the appearance of the pigskin grafts on my upper extremities, they were baffled by my worsening condition. I had begun feeling progressively more ill as time passed, drifting into a foggy mental state with intermittent temperature spikes. All of my extremities, my back, and my trunk were aching, even though I wasn't moving at all.

After I left the tank room, the residents ordered several diagnostic tests, and I was soon being wheeled through the bowels of the hospital again to different divisions of the radiology department. Fortunately, I had not eaten for more than twelve to fourteen hours, as the first procedure was a gastrointestinal study to confirm that all internal connections were intact, ruling out possible leaks since surgery.

Rolling over the cement floors once more through a succession of tunnels and corridors rattled my body, flaring pain from the open sores on my back. I'd start to drift away into a light slumber only to be jolted back by another clatter of the gurney, or by a nurse or tech prompting me to move here or there throughout the gamut of tests. It was like sleep-deprivation torture, nodding off only to be suddenly startled to a semiconscious state, never obtaining a moment of rest or relief. My anxiety increased incrementally, taking me ever closer to the edge of insanity.

From room to room, the gloomy surroundings left me with a suffocating sense of lethargy mixed with a certainty that each new person I met was part of a conspiracy intent on keeping me from drifting into an eternal, dream-filled sleep. I was instructed to perform another series of bodily rolls and twists with the assistance of a technician whose passive attitude suggested that he, like me, was elsewhere in his mind. *God, please grant me patience and tolerance.* After a collection of scans and more X-rays, followed by ultrasound examinations of the veins in my legs, we began the trek back to the burn unit.

By the time we returned, my orderly's shift had ended, so he had passed me off to the night shift guy. It was now after 7:00 p.m. and we had missed the doctors on evening rounds. After all we'd endured, it appeared that we'd have to wait through the weekend before hearing the results.

I'd been praying for patience and tolerance; perhaps I should have been more careful about what I asked for, I realized. *Looks like now I have the perfect opportunity to practice these virtues.*

14

THERAPY

The results of all the tests turned out to be inconclusive, but my body began to bounce back. It was by no means the last time I caused the doctors some alarm, though. On several more occasions through the many weeks I was in the hospital my body would suddenly react as though I had contracted some kind of infection. On more than a few of those occasions, I had.

Once blood is tainted with bacterial or viral contaminants, all bets are off regarding the ensuing battle. Somehow, I found the strength and stamina to keep up the fight. My blood pressure and cardiac output would dip as my heart fatigued from its efforts to compensate for the added stress. And then there were the seemingly constant but irregular temperature spikes. Temperature elevation as a symptom is *sensitive* to many possible causes but it's *specific* to identification of none. While keeping the medical staff on their toes, unfortunately it also mandates an obligatory, sometimes laborious search for corroborating evidence to identify the cause and determine the treatment.

On several nights the medical team kept vigilant watch over me as I hovered on the edge of a crisis. Later, I was told that there were several times when I was "circling the drain," with my prognosis far from certain.

The variable courses of antibiotics, together with further rounds of debridements and tankings, began to take its toll on my precarious yo-yo progress. I could feel my mental brightness dimming. I had many more periods like that afternoon in radiology, with temperature surges inducing delirious hallucinations along with a generalized malaise. Rarely getting more than three hours of sleep at a time, I would awaken to a bizarre, distorted sense of reality, disoriented to place, date, time, or all three. And of course, once again I'd be whisked off for another diagnostic test or procedure.

There were countless trips to radiology or nuclear medicine for more X-rays of some body part or cavity. In my weakened state, it was increasingly hard to follow even the simplest instructions let alone comply with the particular positioning demands of a certain scan or view. Oftentimes I just wanted to be left alone, to fade off to sleep, or at least to fall into some kind of nocturnal state. But the best I could manage was a lethargic zone of restless agitation, never sleeping quite long enough to recharge my depleted energy stores.

From a medical standpoint, physical, occupational, and sometimes speech therapy all have vital roles in the management and restoration of burn patients. The critical importance of maintaining and optimizing function and mobility cannot be overstated.

PTs and OTs are key members of the medical team who assist the doctors in determining the amount of burn involvement, documenting the depth and area of injury. In addition to performing therapeutic exercises, the therapists also design and fabricate, then apply, custom splints to optimize and maintain limb positions where the primary goal is the prevention of contractures.

My therapists had fashioned splints to be worn on my hands, elbows, and ankles at night or whenever I was in bed. They were definitely not comfortable. I even had a pair of "airplane" splints constructed for my shoulders, which made me look like a Cessna 172 aircraft ready for takeoff.

So many professionals extended grace to this often truculent teenager. On the job since day one, no one better embodied the fine balance of firmness and gentleness that was needed to coax and coach me through such a tumultuous journey than Mary, one of the PTs. With her natural charisma, she managed to combine an affable nature with a don't-mess-with-me attitude. She was sure of herself in a matter-of-fact sort of way—a royal queen dictator of her own kingdom. And I was one of her subjects.

"Hi! I'm Mary, your physical therapist," she said with a guileful grin on our first meeting. She was commanding if not demanding, her actions focused and purposeful. At the same time, her gaze reflected warmth and depth, revealing at least a reverence and empathy for my fragile condition as she pressed on.

A tall, trim brunette with short wavy hair parted in the middle, Mary had turquoise eyes that switched to a focused gray, narrowing in anticipation of a task. As my dressings were being removed, she began gently but emphatically grasping my wrist and upper arm with her gloved left and right hands respectively. Mary confidently began raising my arm over my head to seemingly reach toward some point far away and in some other part of the hospital.

Whoa! What's going on? I thought. *Just hold on a second here!* Because of the ventilator, during the first weeks I had been unable to voice more direct objections to her actions, which added pain and stress to an already unbearable procedure. As I grunted, coarse noises from the ventilator tube gagging my throat mercilessly, she went on to explain the merits and vital importance of PT as an additional component to my care plan.

Mary darted quickly around the bed, progressively manipulating each extremity through different movements uniquely characteristic of each joint. She spoke rather casually, but in a monologue, about the glenohumeral, humeroulnar, radioulnar, and carpal joints as though she were introducing the newest flavors of ice cream now available at Baskin-Robbins.

A fter some other "touch up" surgeries, there was another major operation planned before I'd be out of the woods or near stable. This would entail autografting of my own skin to the larger burns on my upper and lower arms and the backs of my hands.

Before transferring new donor skin to recipient areas, surgeons had to cut away the remaining burns and any non-healing eschar or elements left following the pigskin grafting.

Then, most of the remaining unburned skin from my thighs would be harvested; with meshing, surgeons could potentially finish "closing" the majority of the remaining open areas—hopefully in one or two sessions. Finally, a collection of smaller burns on my lower extremities would require further grafting. But the immediate focus was to stop the loss of fluids from the larger wounds, which were always sources of potential infection that could add to my illness, or worse, cause persistent morbidity and even death.

I felt fairly confident that I was much stronger physiologically than I had been on August 13. This stemmed from the knowledge that I'd been privy to during my near-death experience. Ironically, however, other internal data was altered that Friday the thirteenth, resulting in residual fears that could no longer be alleviated by doctors' simple assurances such as, "Don't worry, you'll be asleep and won't feel anything." Thus, I still had some real and justified anxiety, if not acute PTSD, whenever I anticipated general anesthesia or "going under." But trips to the OR continued.

The pain that greeted me upon awakening from the autografting seemed greater than any I had experienced so far because of the extent of the donor sites. It is a cruel twist that healing a bad burn involves creating what is in effect another acute partial thickness burn at the donor site. My thighs and buttocks felt as though they were on fire, having been raided of all remaining normal tissue, essentially skinning me alive. But I knew that I was another step closer to being ready for discharge home.

With few exceptions, patients who have undergone skin grafting operations will say that the most painful aspect is the donor site for several reasons. First, there is the pain of the raw wound itself, which arises from the exposure of raw nerve endings. Then, one of the ways nurses facilitated healing of donor sites when I was a patient was by using a hair dryer to blow hot air directly on them and hasten drying of the soupy wounds. In addition, to potentiate wound contraction, they usually placed an infrared heat lamp over the freshly wet donor site, causing further discomfort as the area dried.

These techniques magnified the burning to well beyond tolerable. Suffice it to say, these lancinating assaults are more than torturous; they're excruciating! As if that's not enough, as the medicated dressings lose all moisture, the wound begins to form a crust-like scab below and within the fine mesh gauze as the surrounding new skin tightens like the head of a drum, stretching the raw edges of the harvest site.

Always keenly attentive to details, Carol, my beloved nurse, made a calendar and posted it on the wall of my room to keep me alert to the passing days of each week. In its margin she listed activities of daily living that I could, should, and eventually would perform independently, according to her. She liked to mark my "grade" for the day, noting such milestones as brushing my teeth, feeding myself, combing my hair, and washing my face. Each Monday she'd enthusiastically post a new list of goals for the week.

The day after she hung the calendar with its list, she had another great idea—that I should begin tolerating progressively longer sessions out of bed and sitting upright in a chair, regardless of the pain it would cause. I barely survived the first goal of ten minutes by flittering my focus between the clock and the bed to which I desperately longed to return. Carol's insistence that I wait out the full ten minutes had me pretty certain that this was the start of a love-hate relationship. I wondered, *What will she add to the list next week?*

As my physiological status progressed from critical to serious and then to good, the time devoted to therapy likewise progressed and increased. Early in my rehabilitative course, therapists employed a tool with which I was quite familiar from my days recovering from Guillain-Barré syndrome: the tilt table. This contraption allowed them to gradually bring my body to a fully erect posture after so many days flat on my back, thus avoiding sudden drops in blood pressure that could cause me to black out.

Not long after I began standing, the nursing team demanded that my chair-sitting sessions be progressively lengthened more aggressively and their frequency increased. In the beginning, each moment in *any* posture other than horizontal felt like an eternity.

Two other people were significant in providing vital therapies during my hospital stay and, in one case, for nearly six months after discharge. Gary was a gentle, red-haired, bearded recreational therapist who engaged me in countless games of Monopoly as we listened to music. He always had a nonjudgmental, attentive ear and was willing to help process any of my fears or concerns—consistently a supportive and loving friend.

Bill B. was a selfless gentleman whom God specially gifted to be a devoted teacher. Sent by the school system for bedside tutoring, Mr. B ensured my ongoing compliance with all academic requirements, especially history and government. He instilled in me a new love for learning that carried me into the following spring when I matriculated back into my junior year and that has remained with me to this day. Mr. B knew how to motivate and inspire me to draw the most from required studies. He always displayed the patience of a saint, instinctively alert to when I needed empathy or was feeling subpar. Some days he'd grade papers as I nodded off, only to resume teaching when I awoke refreshed.

As my seventeenth birthday approached, nearly three months had passed since I had been admitted. I had not only endured exhausting daily therapy but survived more than a half dozen major surgical procedures as well as several more minor ones. So, to boost morale and reward my co-operation, Dr. Frat announced I might be allowed a twenty-four-hour pass to celebrate.

This was far from a given, though. And certainly a permanent discharge seemed out of the question as I was still on IV antibiotics to overcome a recent serious infection of my donor sites. Then there were also numerous open sores in many grafted areas, along with a large and painful wound on my back. Each of these wounds was at significant risk for infection, which would further complicate my ultimate recovery.

In addition to successfully surviving the remaining surgeries, the other concerning issue involved my nutritional status, which was still significantly compromised by the gastric surgery that saved my life on August 13. I would need to consume as many calories as a conditioned Olympic athlete to restore my nutritional health before thinking about any kind of discharge.

Each day I remained on NPO status was another day lost in the vital race to replenish my caloric intake. And I had no excess fat stores to spare: at five feet eight, I weighed under 120 pounds. Because of the hemigastrectomy I was still more than forty pounds below my ideal weight on a good day and had a chronically poor appetite.

So, Dr. Frat was going to allow the twenty-four-hour pass if I could consume three thousand calories per day for one week. To achieve my goal, I began ordering extra entrées, side dishes, and desserts. The old saying about having eyes bigger than one's stomach certainly applied: as much as I wanted to enhance my nutritional status, my limited gastric capacity prevented me from consuming anywhere near enough to reach the seemingly astronomical number needed.

Even allowing for my smaller stomach by eating smaller amounts more frequently during the day, I just didn't feel well enough to eat much. Had I been up to the challenge, it still would have been hard to manage logistically, given the various procedures and therapies that occupied so much of my time awake.

It seemed that the promise of tasting a bit of regular life would remain out of reach. But then I realized evening meal rounds conveniently coincided with visiting hours. Also opportune was that my visitors were usually friends from school—healthy teenagers who had not eaten anything since lunch. They brought with them generous appetites that more than made up for my own limitations.

I'm not sure how much of my sudden eating prowess the medical team truly swallowed. They did infuse a high-calorie milk shake into my stomach every shift through my naso-gastric tube, which only had the self-defeating consequence of further diminishing my appetite. Regardless, my efforts were ultimately applauded when Dr. Frat came by on rounds.

"Well done, Mark," he said with a wink and a knowing grin. "You can go home for your birthday."

It wouldn't actually be home, of course. The house on North Park Drive was still a blackened shell. But I would be going to where Dad and the boys were now settled; it was something of a more permanent situation after several short-term residences and stays. Remarkably, they were living in a house on South Park Drive, which was along the other side of the park, not far from our house on North Park Drive.

On the lookout for a potential rental property that could accommodate them all, Dad had heard about the available house across Bain Park. It had been inherited by a woman whose mother and last surviving parent had died, and it was in the process of being prepared for sale. She was a single woman with no children, an actress who lived primarily in New York City, where she performed intermittently on and off Broadway. As a result, the house on South Park Drive was vacant except for the occasional weekends when she visited while settling the estate.

After visiting me one evening, Dad detoured past the condominium where he and my brothers were temporarily based. He knocked on the front door of the South Park home, which was answered by a woman in her mid-thirties. Standing on the front stoop, he offered an echo of the cold-call pitch that had secured the lot on which he had built our dream home. Dad shared the story of our family, including the tragic deaths of his wife and youngest son in the fire that had also left his eldest son in critical condition in the burn unit at Metro General.

Again, his efforts were persuasive and successful. Not only did Miss Penny Pritchard agree to rent him the property, she accepted his invitation to come with him to visit me on his next trip to Metro. Dad introduced Miss Pritchard to me at my bedside. I did not recognize her but knew that my brothers and I had probably seen or passed her house many times while playing or sledding in Bain Park.

Miss Pritchard had bright blue, penetrating eyes and a warm smile. Her short light brown hair was dusted with some premature gray. Attractive, warm, and intelligent, with a quick wit and a dry sense of humor, she made me feel as though I had known her all my life. Her warmth and compassion highlighted a naturally maternal character that belied the fact that she had no children. She also insisted that I call her Penny, P, or even Pritch, as did her close friends.

I couldn't help wondering, though really doubting, whether anyone on the planet could ever fill the void left by my mother's death. I missed Mom. And I felt bad, maybe even childish, for wanting and needing a mom.

15

PASS

Eager as I was to be allowed home for a day, I was reminded that this was only a brief stop in the long journey that remained ahead. The evening before my twenty-four-hour discharge, I met with Dr. Earle, a plastic and reconstructive surgeon who wanted to discuss some of the surgical procedures I would need in the future.

Dr. A. Scott Earle and his fellow visited my bedside while making rounds. He was a soft-spoken, distinguished-looking, bespectacled gentleman whose reputation preceded him through the accolades showered upon him by nurses, residents, and Dr. Frat himself. He had performed extensive reconstruction on many burn unit patients and was well published in the plastic surgery literature, having been a pioneer in the field of reconstructive surgery as well as surgery of the hand and lower extremities.

Dr. Earle had performed one of the first successful "cross-leg" grafts, saving the lower extremities of a trauma survivor who would otherwise have been a double amputee after being hit by a fast-moving train.

Dr. Earle was approximately six feet tall and balding, with an inquisitive countenance and natural affability. As he and his fellow closely examined my face and hands, he began explaining how much of my appearance could be improved but that it would require multiple and sometimes rather complex surgeries. In fact, he said, they should probably be done over the course of several years, at the end of which I'd be fairly well schooled in the art of plastic surgery. He seemed to be suggesting that maybe someday I should consider going to medical school given the extensive experience I'd be gaining in the field of burn injuries and reconstruction.

But for now, he said, I should remain focused on healing my current burns and skin grafts in preparation for my discharge sometime in the next several weeks. Finally, he smiled and said we'd be meeting again, but probably not until after the start of the new year. After all, it was mid-October and I had a long way to go before I'd be ready to begin thinking about reconstructive surgeries.

After Dr. Earle left my room, I watched as he and his fellow began leading an enormous entourage of residents, nurses, and students out of the burn unit. Sitting there quietly, I began to contemplate my situation, somewhat in awe of the fact that I'd survived such an extensive trauma. At the same time, I began to feel thoroughly overwhelmed with the idea of needing so many more surgeries, not to mention the degree of pain and suffering that was likely in store.

The possibility of ever again having any kind of a normal existence seemed like a fantasy. I wanted to scream or sob but could barely summon the energy to breathe; I felt the walls closing in, like I was being smothered beneath a pile of pillows. Then I remembered the message I'd absorbed during my near-death experience: the road ahead would be trying. I was alive, but it was still difficult to visualize anything but the ever-present deficiencies that remained. I took a brief inventory.

The fingers on both of my hands had developed severe contractures that left them in claw-like deformities. Also, the dorsal surfaces of each hand were developing thick hypertrophic scars, giving them an ugly appearance resembling alligator hide. It didn't take much before I began projecting that my future was doomed. I was paralyzed by fear and the onset of disheartening self-pity.

My shoulder and elbow range of motion were restricted by 60 and 40 percent respectively, and I still had large open areas. I was beginning to develop unsightly deforming scars on my chin and neck that also interfered with normal movement and facial expression. Additionally, parts of my face, chest, and other areas had still not healed; those that had healed lacked normal pigmentation, devoid of typical color or appearance. I could hardly bear to look at myself naked—a far cry from my pre-injury state of a couple months ago, swimming off Florida's beaches in my cutoff shorts.

Dr. Earle's visit had left me with mixed emotions. I was elated about the twenty-four-hour holiday from the unit, but was fearful that I'd be on my own except for help from Dad, Penny, and my brothers. One of the conditions of the rental agreement had been that Penny could use the house's second-floor guest room on her occasional weekends back in Cleveland. I'd grown rather fond of her and was pleased that she'd agreed to come back for the weekend of my temporary discharge.

Prior to my release, the nurses gave Dad detailed instructions on doing my dressing changes. He enlisted Penny to help with everything, which she seemed more than willing to do. It goes to show how Dad and I especially had become attached to her in such a short time—my brothers too. Perhaps she was also warming up to us, though I was convinced she was a genuinely gracious person with a giving heart.

I still did not have the balance or physical strength needed to take a shower, and I needed assistance with sponge baths and the routine activities of daily living: brushing my teeth, getting dressed, eating—even using the bathroom, which was humiliating. Along with the functional restrictions of my upper extremities, movement of everything else was limited by pain and tightness due to grafts or contractures.

The nurses continued their teaching, emphasizing that after all of the wounds were cleaned, dressings placed, and moisturizer applied to any dry areas, my arms and legs were to be wrapped with Ace bandages until I got my custom-fit Jobst garments. Compression of the extremities enhanced circulation while decreasing some of the itching and dryness associated with healing.

This twenty-four-hour pass would prove to be a good test for my family, ensuring their ability to assist with my care after discharge. The entire process to prepare me for a regular day could easily take four hours or more. If either my caregiver or I were not in the proper state of mind, the distance between calm and collected and total chaos was minimal. The psychological disposition of any day was as fragile as fine china.

After ensuring that Dad could handle everything, we were loaded with supplies for twenty-four hours and sent on our way. Hospital procedure required that I leave the building by wheelchair, but I didn't have the strength or endurance to walk even if I had wanted to.

My balance was poor at best, and it was important that I avoid any kind of fall, which would risk tearing my new grafts or shearing scar tissue. Given my overall weakness and the contractures of my clawed hands, I was helpless to break a fall. The resulting setback would be tremendously painful physically and mentally; it had to be avoided at all costs.

Finally, I was cautiously loaded into the car and ready for the ride home.

Having spent months functioning at a snail's pace within the protected walls of the burn unit, the rapidity of things outside the hospital was disorienting. As Dad exited the parking lot I wanted to yell, "Slow down!" Our speed of 15 mph felt like 50 mph: the whole world appeared to be moving by me at warp speed. As we merged with traffic on the interstate, I had to close my eyes to prevent vertigo from sending me into a tailspin.

After nearly a quarter year of confinement, I was the unsuspecting victim of extreme sensory overload. Just watching the world spin by and around me was exhausting. Sudden shifts startled me. At the slightest stimulus I reflexively flinched or shuddered, provoking pain in one part of my body or another as I attempted to reach beyond my limited range of motion. And nothing had prepared me for how much energy and effort each volitional activity required.

The ride home took about forty minutes, most of which I spent staring into my lap with the car seat partially reclined. It was the only way I knew how to subdue the excessive stimuli coming at me with seemingly extreme speed and volume.

As we approached our neighborhood and North Park Drive, there was an ominous, quiet stillness within the car. I'm sure each of us was thinking of whether we should drive by the old McDonough house or go beyond our street and turn onto South Park Drive, which was Penny's street. The collective silence and chill seemed to influence Dad's decision to choose the latter route.

As we slowly exited the car in Penny's driveway, I was amazed by yet another example of how God created such a small world. Were it not for the tree-filled woods of Bain Park, I could have looked nearly due north from her front porch to my family's home. I was incredulous to think that for so many years I lived so close to someone who was now having such a significant influence on my family and me.

I was grateful that, as much at my request as Dad's, Penny was in town the day of my twenty-four-hour escape from the burn unit. As we walked slowly through the breezeway and into the four-bedroom Cape Cod, it had that smell of Grandma's house—a mixture of warmth, home cooking, winter days, and lilacs. Everyone was eager to give me a tour of their home—our home—and the individual spaces in which they were defining some sort of new identity.

They showed me the master bedroom that was being held for me. Dad's room was conveniently across the hall so that he could be ready to help me face each day, and we shared the bathroom between us.

Tim and Dan showed me the basement, which they had converted into their own abode away from home—and otherwise supervising eyes. They told me how they hung out here with their friends, listening to records by Led Zeppelin, Blue Oyster Cult, ELO, Lynyrd Skynyrd, and Boston. Here they also held their own band practices free from outside interference.

Packy showed me his private pad on the second story. It was at the end of a long hallway just beyond another door to the guest room, which was reserved for Penny's use when she was in town. Packy's room was unique, with canted ceilings and north-facing dormers that overlooked Bain Park and its forest of trees—the only things obscuring an otherwise clear view toward our former house bordering the woods on North Park Drive.

The tour complete, I just wanted to catch my breath. I was aware of a growing pile of emotions that needed to find their place. After less than two hours "on the outside," I was quickly aware that this seemingly insignificant twenty-four-hour pass was a new kind of scary.

Do I have what it's going to take, physically and emotionally, to meet this challenge? I wondered. *Of course I do. I must. I will. I will . . . with God's help.*

After settling in, it was nearly time for dinner, naturally preceded by a brief happy hour. Dad offered me a beer, which I eagerly accepted. It had been more than two and a half months since I felt that familiar buzz from alcohol; I was looking forward to it. What I had not expected was something that thoroughly excited me: the constant, unrelenting pain and tightness associated with any movement of my trunk or extremities began to dissipate by the end of that first beer.

Beyond the contracting nature of healing or burn wound closure, one of the most miserable and often debilitating factors for burn survivors is a constant pinching, burning, and itching that occurs as scar tissue dries then stretches, essentially with any movement.

By the end of that first beer, and for the first time since August 3, I began to feel relaxed. The alcohol dulled my perception of the pain that persisted in the background. It also felt as though my movements were more fluid and my gait was smoother, with less stiffness and rigidity. It was such a relief to feel relief!

After a nice dinner with the boys, I sat with Dad and Penny. Although feeling comfortable, I was conscious of the brevity that limited my overnight pass. With this thought, or perhaps because we discussed some of my future surgeries, I found myself slipping back into somewhat of a depression. This was no good: I asked Dad for another beer and we agreed to defer further medical talk while enjoying my liberation from the unit.

That night I slept soundly in my usual post-injury position—prone on my stomach with my head turned to one side and my arms at my sides. Dad reminded me that before the fire I'd often slept with my arms overhead and my hands below the pillow. But now the tightness and contractures restricted my shoulder flexion to slightly more than half of full range of motion, preventing me from being able to sleep with my hands above my head.

This limited mobility also meant that I could not put on a jacket or shirt without assistance. But at least the sedating effects of the beer I drank allowed me to sleep through the night without the usual interruptions associated with pain, itching, or generalized anxiety. Unfortunately, all those symptoms and disturbing sensations welcomed me upon awakening the following morning. The benefits of alcohol had only been temporary.

Dad seemed to be in good spirits, doing well to put his best self forward. I could tell he was anxious about helping me with washing and changing my dressings. First, we enjoyed poached eggs on toast, a favorite of all the McDonough men. It was nearing 10:00 a.m. as he reminded me we were due back at the hospital by 4:00 p.m. and had better get started.

By one o'clock we began wrapping my arms and legs with Ace wraps, which took another forty-five minutes to complete adequately. They had to be wrapped with just the right amount of tension and overlap to avoid restricting circulation or causing skin blisters. Thankfully Dad exhibited more patience than I, as internally I was struggling with the idea of having to return to what I thought of as the burn prison. I tried to remain positive but was quickly becoming exasperated by the reality of everything and longing for some way to escape.

Finally, after all of the "nursing" tasks were finished, I rested in a comfortable rocker in the living room as the clock approached two. I began reflecting on what I'd survived and overcome but also on the challenges and potential obstacles that yet awaited. It felt like I was traveling through a snowstorm while looking out the rear window. I could see where I'd been from the tracks in the snow, but I was afraid to look forward into the blinding flurries rushing toward the windshield. I was desperately trying but failing to feel secure with the blurry picture of the road ahead. There's a fine line between disregarding the present and what *is* and being stuck in the future—focused fearfully and intently on what *may be*. Yet there was nothing I could do to change either one.

As I headed back to Metro with Dad and Penny, the Cleveland weather mirrored my mood. The gray sky was heavy with low-hanging nimbus clouds that needed only to burst with a downpour to complete the gloomy scene. Despite my persistent efforts to wear the smothering garments of my dismal world loosely, I just couldn't keep at bay a sadness like homesickness. It brought to mind a summer when I was eight, and Mom and Dad had left my brothers and me at the St. Christopher summer camp for a second session. It was an overwhelming sentiment of loneliness. On course for another petulant argument with God, I stared out the window quietly. Inside, my mind was whirring. *Why did this have to happen to me? Why can't I be healed and go home permanently? It's all so unfair, God. Why?*

After ten minutes or so of brooding silence, Dad tried to console me. He knew me so well.

"It's going to be okay, chum," he said. "We knew it would be hard returning after a twenty-four-hour visit home, right? It shouldn't be too long now until you're discharged for good."

I appreciated Dad's valiant effort to encourage me, though he couldn't quite hide a tone of sympathetic frustration. His attempt to be positive gave me a pang of guilt. I should be grateful for my family and for the many friends who had been so supportive. But somehow the day at "home" in Penny's house, across the park from our destroyed home, had heightened my awareness of all that had been lost. Physically, mentally, emotionally, the overnight visit had left me exhausted.

From the visitors' parking lot, Dad wheeled me, per hospital protocol, into an elevator and up to the 11 West floor. I was back. Dad seemed somewhat anxious to get home; business required him to travel to Boston the following morning and he still had to pack. His partners had been sympathetic, but now, nearly three months after the fire, they were expecting more of him again. I knew Dad felt guilty, trapped, and powerless to alter the circumstances. But his haste to leave only added to my peevish attitude. Wallowing in my self-centeredness, I did nothing to alleviate his sense of shame. I was too focused on the negative.

Eventually, I tried to appear more cheerful, understanding that he was sad at having to say good night with me feeling so disheartened. After hugs from him and Penny, I sat in an armchair at the bedside in my room and watched them leave.

Leaning back in my seat, I tried to raise my right leg, planning to rest it on the bedside table. Instead I slammed it on the surface in anger. I winced, uttering a grunt of agony and annoyance at myself, especially knowing I still had a large pressure ulcer on that heel. Shooting pain radiated up to my hip.

Just perfect! I thought, feeling sorry for myself.

Sometime later a nursing assistant came into the room to fill my water pitcher.

"Is there anything I can do?" she asked.

"No," I replied curtly. "There's nothing anyone can do!"

I thought back to my experience in the operating room, the absolute assurance and confidence of being in God's presence. *How can he love me, or anyone, and allow us to experience such tragedy?*

Intellectually, I knew my sentiments were not in concert with my beliefs and faith. But such knowledge was overshadowed by doubts and insecurities. And the path from my head back to my heart seemed blocked. I felt threatened by paralyzing fear, suffocation, and a hopeless feeling of desperation. I was frustrated beyond measure. I believed God was real, but any prior clarity was dulled; I found it so hard to trust his plan.

This hopelessness accounted for a sudden and chilling pall of sadness that was descending upon my world, narrowing my perspective and confounding my reality. The only saving grace was that I *knew* I needed to be rescued from my self-destructive mentality. There was a tug-of-war going on inside.

As my right heel continued to throb, I cried out, "God, if you're really on my side, I need help!"

16

FAITH

Drawn, heaving sobs. They came from somewhere deep inside, a part of me untapped for years. As my lower lip quivered, my hands trembled on the arms of the chair and the small pouch that was my stomach began to clench. I wept raw and hard for the first time since I was a young boy.

Sure, there had been tears along the way, but they had been fleeting and light, a swiftly evaporating response to a small injury or frustration. These were big, welling up from some unseen reservoir deep within, waiting for this moment. They streamed down my cheeks, my body convulsing in spasms that left me coughing and choking as though I had a bad case of hiccups.

The intensity left me aching for Mom, to have her there, to have her soothe me and tell me that everything was going to be all right.

But it may never be, I thought. *Everything just hurts so much. I want Mom and Toby back, here with me. I want my old body back, the way it used to be. It's all so much to accept. I never signed up for all of this. God, how could you let this happen? And what's wrong with me?*

Hoarse from having been connected to the breathing tube for so long, the noises coming from my throat sounded like a blend between a hacking cough and the barking, wounded cry of a dying animal. I was sure I would be overheard, but I couldn't suppress the flood of emotions. My torso and extremities continued to shudder in a paroxysm. I was certain the elegiac fits of frustration would attract unwanted attention.

As the emotional volcano began to subside, my heaving eased and I began to breathe a little more easily as the aftershocks followed. Then I continued to sob, more silently now. I could feel my pulse starting to slow, as though someone had taken their foot off my heart's accelerator. Then I saw him. He seemed to appear suddenly from nowhere.

Dr. Frat was standing quietly in the doorway to my room. I was surprised to see him there, his stethoscope poking out of the side pocket of his white lab coat. It was now well after 8:00 p.m., past his typical departure time—if there really is such a thing for someone in charge of a major hospital division like the burn unit. I now realize he was making "stealth rounds," the vehicle by which attending doctors check up on their patients without a cadre of residents in tow needing answers and instruction. It was also a means by which doctors could spend some uninterrupted time with their patients.

Although I knew he had probably witnessed my crying spell, I did not feel embarrassed. Something about his empathetic look put me at ease.

Without speaking, Dr. Frat moved closer, standing at my side as I sat semi-slumped in my chair. Then he gently placed his hand on my shoulder, holding fast as my body continued to quiver while the tears gradually subsided. After a few silent minutes that felt like many more, he said, "I gather being home and with your family was enjoyable but you're not happy being back here." I stood up from my chair, awkwardly bracing myself and balancing with one hand's curled fingers around the wooden end of the armrest.

"I'm not really happy being anywhere right now," I said reticently.

Before I could turn to sit on the edge of my bed, Dr. Frat replied, "How about a hug?" I immediately became tearful again and timorously tried to reach my arms around him as he continued, "You know, things can only get better. Seriously, you've quite miraculously survived a nearly fatal war, along with countless triumphs in many battles along the way."

On top of the physical exertion, and exhausted by the preceding twenty-four hours at home, the internal stress of the last few minutes left me spent. Ending the embrace, I maneuvered onto my bed, elevating its head and lying back against the pillow. As I did, the gauze dressing from the large open area on my back sheared away, the spike of pain adding a final reminder of my misery.

When my breath and heart rate were steady once more, the words began to tumble out.

"I don't care very much, to be honest, Dr. Frat," I said. "What's the use of winning a war if *this* is the life that I am fighting for? I'm not sure that it's worth the effort."

Dr. Frat just stood quietly at my bedside, carefully filling and packing his pipe. I could smell the tobacco wafting in the air; it evoked the safe and familiar feeling I'd always known with Grandpa Hardman, Mom's dad, also a pipe smoker.

After a silent respite, I tried to justify the reasons for my anger and dismay. I poured out my heart, explaining that I knew God had a plan, but in this moment it just didn't make any sense to me. I couldn't see the path ahead; the details were blurred and confused. I should be positive and determined, I recognized, as I knew that my heavenly encounter had been real. I sincerely wanted to know and feel that certainty again. I explained how I just couldn't shake myself free from a sense of futility and unfairness. Moreover, I was powerless in trying to find my way out of this depressing hole. "Why must it all hurt so much?" I asked him. "Why would God let us suffer like this?"

He waited until my stream of words ran out. When he spoke, it was with a gentle tone, evidence of his great empathy.

"Oh, Mark, I understand your frustration," Dr. Frat told me. "And I grieve with you in your pain, as well as that of so many others in this world who will continue to suffer unimaginable trials and hardships up until—and often including—death. But I also know that one of the positive aspects of struggling through such pain is that it reminds us that God sent us his Son to know and understand our pain, and to suffer for us. You've been through more than your share of turmoil, but we're reminded that he is by our side through any and all struggles we endure on this planet."

I listened intently as he continued.

"God doesn't want to see you in such agony any more than you want to be in it. But he wants to be the source for the strength you need to overcome this devastating challenge—and overcome it you will, with his help. But you have free will to accept or reject that help."

This was not Dr. Frat the burn expert but Dr. Frat the believer. "What I do know for certain," he said, "is that believing he knows the reasons and the plan is the only way I can continue doing what I do here." He gestured to the unit behind him. "I can't do anything without him."

Dr. Frat spoke about how some people get stuck harboring resentments, exhausting themselves over things of the past that they don't understand. Something started to stir inside me. I knew what it was like to have no energy left to do anything. *Why waste those precious resources on things that aren't going to change anything? Why not invest that limited energy or strength in something real, positive, and in the here and now, not in a past that cannot be changed?*

We talked on, Dr. Frat encouraging me to keep asking God for the faith to keep believing and trusting even when I didn't understand.

"So, I guess that faith is believing that God does have a plan and a purpose even though we can't see the whole picture," I said. Suddenly I felt a chill rush through my body, aware again of the giddy certainty, the sense of mirth I'd known on the operating table that frightening day when everything *had* made sense. I could feel the corners of my mouth turn up slightly toward a smile.

Then Dr. Frat said something that would become a pivotal moment not only in my recovery from my injuries but for the rest of my life.

"You simply need to see the glass as being half full instead of half empty," he offered. "Remember when I came into your room, and I said that things can only get better?"

I nodded with a sense of excitement, energized but still apprehensive. He continued, "Well, things can always get worse, of course; it's all relative. But our subjective assessment depends on the perspective we choose to maintain. By mentally striving to focus on the positive aspects of our experiences instead of the relatively negative aspects, we will continue to realize a reality of progressively positive or constructive, confirming events."

I warmed to the wisdom, but I couldn't resist playing devil's advocate.

"Yeah, but you said it yourself: everything is relative."

Dr. Frat wasn't offended. He smiled and said, "Thank you for making my point! Yes, everything is relative—which is all the more reason to fix our gaze toward the positive or best extreme in any situation, Mark."

He went on, "You're free to see the glass as half empty, continually reminding yourself and others of everything the fire took away from you. You can focus on the loss of your mom and your brother, or the loss of some of your beautifully tanned skin. Or you can choose to keep your sights on the progress you're making each day, along with the priceless spiritual experience and newly acquired strength and wisdom you've come to realize.

"It nearly cost you your life, after all: why not make the best of what is or what will be? It's definitely more constructive and productive than focusing on the pain you've endured or the losses you have sustained."

I felt as though some internal puzzle pieces were finally being put into place. I told Dr. Frat how during my near-death experience I had realized that the truth is always evident if we're sincere in our quest to find it. Then we can invest our unexpended resources in holding on to or accepting that which we know to be true.

Dr. Frat encouraged me to continually ask God for the faith to believe. I was instantly filled with gratitude as I recognized this divinely orchestrated reminder of what I'd seen so clearly on August 13, as if coming fully awake at last.

I was vividly reminded of a message or theme that was clearly represented that day in the operating room. "Faith is believing that God does have a plan and a purpose even though we can't see the whole picture," I reiterated to Dr. Frat. "In fact, we're not equipped to begin grasping what he knows. It's quite complex yet simple in a way."

Someday, I thought, *once again he'll reveal the entire scenic landscape, and once again it will seem so obviously simple that we'll belly laugh in euphoric bliss.* It was the same feeling I'd been aware of during my unique adventure that day in surgery.

Remarkably, this wonderful feeling had been immediately preceded by the most terrifying of events: awaking midway through the operation, suffering every cut, unable to move a muscle. Yet eventually I was able to realize the whole picture and it was picture perfect. There certainly did seem to be a kind of recurring pattern here—a message that trumped all others brilliantly. Yet something was missing.

"Dr. Frat, ever since my experience in the operating room that day I have known that God is real—1,000 percent real. So why am I doubting anything?"

He smiled again, recalling when I had first recounted my near-death experience to him. "Perhaps you no longer have the ability to see the whole mosaic that God sees," he suggested. Perhaps not staying there with Mom and Toby, remaining alive to complete some unfinished business, required losing some of the awareness of the big picture.

"He wants you to continue nurturing your relationship with him by seeking the truth."

In that moment, as Dr. Frat stood serenely at the foot of my bed, a blanket of peace and certitude settled over me. It wasn't Mom speaking, but somehow I just knew that everything was going to be all right.

It was 10:30 p.m. when Dr. Frat finally wished me a good night and left my room. When he had arrived, I had been anxious and distraught, on the edge of an emotional cliff, ready to jump. Now I had stepped back, turning in a new direction. The way ahead would not be easy, I knew; but it would be worth it, and I wouldn't be alone.

I lay peacefully in my bed listening to music from the small radio built into the bed remote. There were more tears, but this time they brought relief rather than just sadness. They seemed to wash away some of the heartache—not completely out of view, but into a ravine bordering my path, alongside the jagged boulders of doubt that together would have otherwise blocked me from moving forward.

I awoke the next morning with an almost tangible lightness. The previously compressing load that had settled somewhere over my chest had been lifted. I felt naked—emotionally raw and vulnerable. Perhaps this is what it meant to have an open heart? *The lurking fears that hide in dark shadows never seem so huge when they're exposed to light.*

For the first time that I could remember, and certainly since my admission to the hospital, I had slept well. It was not uninterrupted, but the few moments of wakefulness were brief and I had drifted restfully to sleep again quickly. As I reflected on the previous evening's encounter, I realized that Dr. Frat's unscheduled appearance at my door had been the answer to my anguished prayer for help.

I was touched by his concern, by the time he had so generously given to me. Simply telling me to "Hang in there, Mark" and moving on to his next patient would have been entirely acceptable, yet he had gone so much further, taking the time to patiently reveal something of himself to me—something of the man within that made him the strong doctor without.

Many burn survivors become comfortable or complacent through their dependence on the unit's nurses and staff, making transition to the outside world difficult. They can also feel protected by the privacy and familiarity of the hospital where few, if any, are surprised by the scarring or disfigurement of those with a major burn injury.

Like many who have reason to deviate from or are born different from the norm, survivors of a major burn face a lifelong struggle with reconciling their self-image with the profile they present to others. If they feel rejected by others, with or without cause, it becomes increasingly difficult to accept themselves. But Dr. Frat saw that I was determined and ready to face the world, especially following our discussion and affirmations that evening. My self-esteem and confidence were on their way back.

To my delight, Dr. Frat finally determined an initial but official discharge week from the hospital, which he anticipated to be around the beginning of November. The designation "initial" was significant, as that discharge would be the first in a series of many discharges that would follow due to ongoing reconstructive surgeries.

On Friday, November 5, 1976, ninety-five days after I had been wheeled in on a gurney, my friend Roosevelt, the transportation technician with whom I had taken many trips around the hospital, pushed me by wheelchair out of the unit and into the visitor elevators, and we descended to the main lobby.

Having achieved the many goals set by countless doctors, nurses, and therapists, along with a few of my own, I was officially discharged from the burn unit on 11 West. As we exited, several members of the burn unit staff followed us down to the ground floor to say goodbye.

Dad had gone ahead to bring the car around to the portico. As we wheeled up alongside the car, I looked up to an ominously gray sky. A low-lying layer of cumulonimbus clouds was unable to fully shield a vermilion sky as it moved slowly to the east and blanketed the near-west side of Cleveland. There was a fresh, crisp chill in the air and that ever-present fall scent of burning leaves. It had been summer when I arrived. I was truly leaving the hospital to a new season: literally by the calendar, figuratively as I ventured into a new phase of a drastically altered life.

Waving to well-wishing staff as we pulled away, I felt a hot flash of emotions. I rolled the passenger window partway open to savor the autumn fragrances carried in by an early boreal breeze. I thought about how I'd traveled home from other hospitals twice before with Mom, once following my birth and again while still recovering from GBS.

Not this time. Her absence, and Toby's, cast a dreary haze on the day, not unlike the clouds overhead. I looked hopefully forward to the radiance that, for now, was hiding behind their cover.

17

PHOENIX

If we all gave a collective sigh of relief that I was home again, the gasp that quickly followed was but an intimation of the daunting pilgrimage we'd begun.

Dad and the boys were always supportive, helping me in every way possible. In fact, it often seemed like most events revolved around me, and it wasn't long before I was cowled in a cloud of guilt. I worried that my brothers would start to resent me, tired of hearing "Mark needs this" and "Mark needs that." I knew they were confronting their own scars from the fire, hidden as they were, without having to suffer the demands of their invalid brother.

Tim and Dan were close enough in age to be supportive of one another, but Packy often seemed to be cut adrift. Five years younger than Dan and without Toby, his younger brother-in-arms, he was frequently lost within the shuffle of a busy household.

This was exacerbated by Dad's having to focus so much of his attention on me, either directly helping me or ensuring that someone else could and did. I continued my home studies with Mr. B in hopes of matriculating back into school, and returned to the hospital three times a week for physical and occupational therapy. The outpatient rehabilitation required transport to and from the hospital—a twenty-five-minute drive each way every Monday, Wednesday, and Friday. I'd have an hour each of PT and OT, then return home for more tutoring.

Outwardly, we all made the best of the difficult situations and circumstances, each adjusting to his new place and space in the family. The months following my discharge were full of many firsts, especially without Mom and Toby in the picture. Christmas was one of the bigger ones. Six weeks post-discharge, we drove to Columbus, Ohio, to spend several days with Dad's sister Marsha and our cousins. Being away from our own home and so many painful reminders seemed like the best way of coping with the inevitable melancholy of holiday memories.

On the drive to southern Ohio, Dad forsook his usual favorite radio station, allowing us to introduce and enlighten him to the life-affirming R & B–influenced rock that we enjoyed.

"Okay, you guys," he said. "You can play whatever you want, but you've got to explain the meaning or the words, fair enough?" So we'd interpret the lyrical intentions of classic artists like Led Zeppelin, Eric Clapton, or The Who, inspiring some thoughtful discussions.

The trip was enjoyable but also quite stressful. Traveling while continuing to heal meant managing my dressings and

Ace wraps without the familiarity and welcome privacy of home. I was rather self-conscious at first and constantly wore long-sleeved shirts, uncomfortable with letting others see the extent of my injuries and scars.

Dad assumed the dual roles of patriarch and matriarch while trying to find ways to keep the family machine running. He was nothing short of amazing in the ways he adapted to change, at least by outward appearances. In alliance with us, he attempted to connect at new levels, buying his first pair of bell-bottom Levi's for the trip—a far cry from his typical khaki slacks and loafers. To others he maintained a brave and courageous front, indomitably steadfast.

The new year brought fresh challenges. I had been looking forward to receiving my Jobst garments, the specially tailored compression suits intended to replace the Ace bandages with which I'd been wrapping my extremities every day. Woven with a special elastic fabric, the garments were intended to provide a firm, even pressure over my burn-scarred arms, legs, and trunk. They would also fit over the gauze dressings still being applied to open burns on my back and right ankle.

The Jobst jacket and leggings had been individually measured for me like a bespoke suit, and I was anxious to don them, having brought the items home from my latest physical therapy session. Dad and I knew they'd economize the time spent getting me ready every morning while providing better anti-scarring compression.

However, since leaving the hospital I had gained back some of the weight I lost during the three-plus months in the burn unit. I was still some thirty pounds below the ideal weight for my height and build, but I had gained enough to compromise the fit of the new skintight apparel, worn like underwear.

We had been instructed to expect that the garments would be tight but would stretch with time. Accordingly, Dad was determined to get them on me despite the seemingly Herculean magnitude of the task; it was much like getting an elephant into a turn-of-the-century corset.

Within minutes, the sleeves of the jacket began to restrict my blood flow and my hands were tingling and numb. The jacket's zipper began to cut into my abdominal skin and midline scar, prompting me to voice a chorus of cuss words. Likewise, Dad began to direct pointed insults at the garment along with a few colorful expletives of his own. Moments later the pressure from the zipper cut through the underlying skin, and blood began to seep through the taut nylon fabric over my abdomen and back.

That was the last straw. Dad tried to unzip the jacket several times, but to no avail as the increased tension on the zipper precluded normal function. Finally, he grabbed a pair of sharp bandage scissors from the nearby dresser and cut through the exorbitantly expensive garment from bottom to top, and up both sleeves. My torso and extremities sprang from their confinement like croissant dough from a canister or a Jack from its box: "Pop goes the weasel!"

So much for the convenience of custom garments and not having to deal with Ace wraps. Because of my continued weight gains, I never did get measured for a new jacket for my upper body and continued using the Ace wraps instead. The leotard pants, however, seemed to fit well. Overall, we continued with some form of compression for most of the year post-injury, after which most doctors agree little further benefit is likely.

Early in 1977 I was readmitted to the hospital for the first of what would be a lengthy series of reconstructive surgeries. So began a seemingly regular cycle of two weeks in the hospital for surgery and recuperation, then time back home to finish healing, adjust to the latest procedure, and anticipate the next admission.

Like the fabled phoenix, I had risen from the ashes. Mirroring my own story, the fable tells of this mythical bird's flight from the first rosebush in the garden of paradise. It is said that the phoenix was struck down by the flaming sword of a cherub, later rising from the ashes to be more beautiful in song and colorful plumage than ever before. The cherub's sword became the surgeon's scalpel. With healing, time, and the grace of God, I would rise up to become a renewed version of myself, physically and mentally. Certainly, my plumage would be more colorful too.

For each operation, going under anesthesia was an opportunity to further fortify my foundation of faith, embracing the confidence gained through my near-death experience.

Many claim that when faith is strong enough, there is no cause for fear. But for me, it was within the context of fear that my quest for faith began. It seemed only natural that I should fear the potentially challenging obstacles ahead or the pain that I expected to confront along the way. Yet, I was learning that I could have those fears while remaining faithful that God would stay nearby if I asked him to, helping me to meet the demands head-on. The true measure of my success was evident in the progressively increasing amount of trust I had that he was there to help me through the process. *Perhaps the gap narrows between what I know will be challenging or painful and the degree to which I rely on his presence and helping strength*, I thought.

Fortunately, the board of education allowed my extensive physical and occupational therapy sessions to substitute for required physical education credits. By the spring I transitioned back into my high school's junior class without deficiencies in educational requirements. My teachers and classmates could not have been more supportive and encouraging throughout the process. I never felt anything but acceptance from my peers.

During these months, my family and I had made some major decisions regarding our house on North Park Drive. Although the fire had claimed the lives of Mom and Toby, we unanimously wanted to live there again. Despite the fire having violently destroyed its interior, no elements could ever destroy the spirit that inspired Dad's dream and everything that had defined us as a family. Our future would always be attached to our history there. While much memorabilia had perished in the early hours of August 3, 1976, none of the memories would ever be extinct.

An official investigation determined the cause of the fire to be an "instant on" television, common in that era. Along with many similar appliances, it contained a feature that would allow it to turn on with little or no warm-up time.

With advice from friends and others, Dad was encouraged to file a lawsuit. But after a yearlong stressful preparation we settled out of court. No monetary compensation could ever suffice for the lives lost, nor the physical and emotional pain.

After legal fees were paid, we were able to begin rebuilding our home and lives.

As with my personal rise from the ashes, we all wanted to see our family home restored more beautifully than ever. We also could not imagine living apart from our neighbors in our Fairview Park community. My brothers and I were intent on finishing school with our friends. We couldn't imagine walking or riding past our former homestead after some other family had restored it to their own particular taste.

That spring, wearing old clothes and masks, Dad and my brothers—along with Penny, the Rattigans, and many close friends and neighbors—gathered at the boarded-shut property on North Park Drive. Together they began the arduous task of going through every room of the house and disposing of unsalvageable remnants and detritus. Empty open-bed trucks were parked in the yard so that items could be thrown out windows into their waiting bins. The few recognizable fragments were residual reminders of the lives that were shaped and grew there since the house was built.

Prior to that day, the house had been shuttered for months while insurance adjusters traversed every square foot, sometimes on hands and knees, assessing the damage and taking a detailed inventory. Often it was only by salvaging smoke-damaged photos that the home's pre-fire contents or condition could be proven for the insurance settlement.

Unable to help with the physical labor, I was there to "supervise" as the others went through the place room by room. Because of the open wounds I had from my latest surgery, I could not risk contamination, or worse, an infection.

The sour, smoky smell clung to everything. I was overwhelmed by the devastation as we walked inside, recalling how I had been trapped when the loving homestead was transformed into a furnace.

"Okay, I've seen enough," I said, stepping outside to wait for the others to finish their inspection.

Penny was a source of many moments of love and laughter. She continued to make frequent visits to Cleveland from New York City, staying in the second-floor spare bedroom of the home that we were renting from her per our agreement.

She and Dad forged a close friendship that lifted his spirits notably. Over time she became a cherished supporter of my family and me as we slowly adapted to our new circumstances. She became a welcome if rare female influence in a household of McDonough men.

Part of Dad's role as VP of an active securities investment firm demanded that he travel out of town. As the oldest son, I would have been left in charge under normal circumstances. But given my current physical limitations, it was clear that we needed some kind of housekeeper. The job requirements were those of caretaker, an adult supervisor to assist with various parental duties when Dad was traveling or in the evenings when he was required to work late.

We weren't completely helpless. Fortunately, Mom had insisted that her five sons become proficient in various home economics skills as well as our regular masculine duties. In addition to maintaining the yard and garage and being responsible for the trash disposal, we boys had each been taught to iron or fold our own laundry, which was placed in designated name-tagged baskets. Mom was quite the taskmaster. She trained us domestically through weekly rotating

schedules where we were responsible for cleaning dishes, setting and clearing the table, making lunches and coffee for the
following day, or assisting with cooking and salad preparation. Some of us could even embroider, sew, and knit, thanks
to Granny McDonough's patient tutelage.

Still, we needed some consistent help; Alice from *The
Brady Bunch* or Uncle Charlie from *My Three Sons* would
have been ideal. We soon discovered that such a candidate
did not exist in the Cleveland area, or likely anywhere else.
Nonetheless, we began a rather comical period of "audition-
ing" individuals for the role—a venture that exposed us to
an entire world of colorful characters, each with their own
issues, personality disorders, and even obsessions.

For example, Mrs. G was a mildly obese, bespectacled
lady with curly blue-gray locks and rosy cheeks who squinted
while smiling a nearly toothless grin. She wore a starched
white nursing uniform around the clock and smacked her
lips constantly, even when not eating. She was much like
a cow chewing its cud, instilling fear in those nearby that
she might cough up a food bolus at any moment. Her approach from another room was always foretold as she had
that "corduroy phenomenon," where her massive nylon-
clad thighs rubbed together as she walked. Several weeks
into Mrs. G's time with us, Dad began to notice a gradual
depletion of his underwear and sock stores. It also seemed
that we were missing a succession of pots, pans, and kitchen
utensils.

Then, one morning, Mrs. G failed to report for duty. Her
absence again the following day became cause for concern.
Failing to reach her by telephone, Dad and Penny made a
visit to Mrs. G's furnished apartment to rule out a possible

medical mishap. They knocked on the door for several minutes before summoning the superintendent for help.

Upon opening the door, they discovered that Mrs. G had apparently vacated the premises in something of a hurry, leaving no details or forwarding address. She had, however, left behind half of our kitchen items; Dad's underwear and socks were hidden beneath her bed.

Another lady, Miss Claire, seemed to fit the bill for a while. Miss Claire dressed formally, with dresses and high-heeled shoes or buckram attire that was hardly the uniform for tackling the disorderly environment of five guys. She was dotty if not obsessed with anything and everything Elvis Presley. She drove a Cadillac and listened exclusively to Elvis's music.

Unfortunately, after Elvis's death in August 1977, she became emotionally fragile, unable to tolerate the demands of her position. When last we heard, she was on her way to Memphis and Graceland.

18

CHOICES

Overall, 1977–78 was a year of rebuilding, with the new construction on our home symbolic of the restoration that was occurring in each of our lives.

Returning to our North Park Drive house sometimes felt like coming home but other times more like moving in, depending on the day and my mood. Coming home mandated a psychological adjustment that at times seemed glacially slow; moving in was a physical task requiring just a few days.

Restoring the entire interior of the house included changing everything—color schemes, wallpaper, carpeting—and even finishing the basement, a project started before the fire. We doubled the size of the family room by removing the exterior wall with its sliding glass doors and closing in the adjacent screened porch. Otherwise, most of the original footprint remained. The formal living room in the front of the house became a billiard parlor with a solid oak pool table surrounded by bar stools with armrests.

Indeed, coming home often felt like the beginning of the second part of our lives. But for the memories, at times it seemed like I was living a different life altogether. Yet in any given moment, something I saw—the bricks or marble, a window or door—could transport me back to a time and circumstances I'd never experience again.

On occasion I'd be in the master bedroom or Toby's old room, acutely aware of the lives that ended there. The associated feelings would leave me forlorn, so overwhelmed that I'd reflexively push them down like packing a musket; sometimes the feelings would descend to almost unreachable depths. I was unaware of their potential for coming back up at some other time or place as part of the healing process.

After the fire, insecurities regarding my physical appearance were magnified for certain. I was self-conscious about my scars, and it would be quite a while before I'd be comfortable in anything other than long-sleeved shirts, sweaters, and turtlenecks. Also, as I continued undergoing reconstructive surgeries on a regular basis, I was often between procedures and sporting bulky dressings or bandages.

My friends and classmates were empathetically supportive of me, at least by virtue of the fact that I was a survivor of a major tragedy in our community. Despite the presence of the usual cliques, I felt comfortable forming friendships with any student across the student body spectrum. My perspective concerning the value of relationships in general changed following the fire. Authenticity became a prized characteristic of friendships. Low on my list of priorities was the acquisition or maintenance of popularity.

This resulted in a much-needed boost in self-confidence. Paradoxically, being self-conscious about my outward appearance became the motivation to trust the personal attributes that defined my inner self.

Unlike many burn survivors, I did not struggle as much with the sense of isolation often imposed by a society that places such emphasis on outward appearance. Spiritually, I felt confident. And it only took one or two positive experiences to instill the self-assurance I needed to pursue more.

Alcohol and other "stuff" also played a part in helping me overcome the inhibitions caused by my burns, though this would prove to be less constructive long-term. In any event, by the time I graduated from high school I had enjoyed several relationships with young ladies that added to my developing self-esteem.

Diane helped me in the early days after the fire. We had been dating casually before that; nothing serious, just hanging out together with our other friends. But she was very supportive, coming to visit me regularly while I was in the hospital and boosting my spirits. One night, when I was running one of the high fevers that would leave me semi-delirious, the result of some kind of infection, I desperately needed to feel some intentional physical affection. I asked Diane if she would mind just laying her head on my chest.

It was a moment of tenderness and raw vulnerability that belied the irony of the moment. Though I was covered in the physical barrier of bandages, Diane's gesture soothed the pain for a while, allowing me to feel that, even with my open wounds, burns, and scars, perhaps I could still be lovable, or at least not repulse someone I desired intimate contact with.

When I returned to high school I dated girls near my age and also experienced some intimacy in those relationships. There were even a couple of surprise encounters with older women, including one reminiscent of the movie *The Graduate*. These went further than they should have, also igniting some internal discomfort. However, they did help restore vital components of an ego that could otherwise have been permanently damaged by the wounds, scars, or other evidence of my injuries. Still, along with the enjoyment I'd derived from the romantic encounters, I carried an unshakable awareness of how God was real, of how much he loved me, and that above everything else, love was the one virtue that should guide my life. Somehow I also knew that my actions fell short of his ways.

In the wake of our tragedy, and despite a faith that had been strengthened by God's hand guiding me through our ordeal, church attendance became even more irregular after Mom's death. I often struggled with the role that religion played in shaping personal morality. But I remained convinced of God's existence and that he had a plan and a purpose for my life.

This wasn't the only internal conflict I was dealing with. I was also wrestling with tensions over where I fit with my friends and what I should do with my future. Part of the struggle had to do with expectations I had for myself—some likely a result of the tragedy, others not unlike those of any teen—along with what I perceived others expected of me.

Yet as I gradually resumed more and more of a regular life, it became increasingly evident that my experiences had in some ways set me apart from many of my peers. Not by choice. I'd simply been forced to confront some issues sooner than I would have otherwise, and in a few ways I lost some of the innocence that might have sheltered or protected me until later in life.

While in no urgency to get there, I was developing a clearer picture of where I wanted to go. Though I remained something of a free spirit outwardly, inside I felt a determination to realize a purpose for my life; this conviction seemed to give me more of an internal drive than I'd have otherwise had.

Before I was born, my mother had a career as a science teacher. So perhaps it was due to her influence that I'd always had an appreciation for biology. Through my frequent returns to the hospital for different therapeutic and surgical procedures, I had acquired a fascination with medical technology and rehabilitation. I talked to the therapists a lot about what they'd been required to study and was amazed at how rigorous their schooling had been. They could name every single part of the anatomy in detail, and their pre–physical therapy training was a match for a premed curriculum.

Some of the therapists and doctors I met, like Dr. Fratianne, were among the most intelligent and admirable people I knew. I respected their character and their demonstrated ability to care. A few, however, had no idea about how to communicate or deal with people. They could tend to the body but overlooked the person, and they all but denied the spirit. I felt particularly sensitive to issues of pain and being dependently at the mercy of others: this was where I felt I could really make a difference and affect a positive change. I began to nurture that notion.

On the home front, Dad began drinking much more heavily. Grieving the loss of his wife and a child, carrying the burden of a convalescing son, trying to solo-parent a family of growing rambunctious boys, and attempting to meet the requirements of a demanding career nearly depleted everything he had.

Loneliness and circumstantial depression were mixed with a genetic predisposition toward alcoholism: the disease had afflicted my Grandpa McDonough during the later years of his life. Also, an older and younger sister of Dad's had both battled drinking—one of them dying in an alcohol-related motor vehicle accident.

Just like before the fire, it became increasingly difficult to maintain a constructive relationship with Dad. Alcohol sparked frequent clashes between him and one or another of us—even with Penny, whose presence we enjoyed more frequently. She and Dad had become fast friends, and gradually she developed a sincere interest in my brothers and me as well.

My own denial likely precluded a clear view through the alcohol haze. Since my twenty-four-hour pass home, I'd become aware that a beer buzz could take the edge off my pain. Self-medicating in this way became routine. As before the fire, weekends consisted of kicking back with my friends, drinking some beer and occasionally smoking weed.

Meanwhile, in keeping with our family's ingrained work ethic, I began thinking about part-time employment. As soon as the doctors granted permission, I was anxious to resume earning money to fund my personal entertainment and continue saving for college.

During my senior year I was employed as a lifeguard at an indoor pool where I didn't have to disrobe. By the spring of that year, I was working as a gas station attendant, where I could even tolerate the labor involved with fixing flat tires or minor auto repairs. I usually wore gloves—part of the custom-fit Jobst garments—to protect my delicate skin from casual trauma. I was determined to do everything possible to prevent my hand injuries from becoming functional limitations or disabilities. After every surgery on either of my hands, I remained vigilantly compliant with any therapeutic exercises so that, with persistence, I always found a way to overcome potential limitations to performing any skill or activity. At home I had resumed playing the piano while Tim jammed on drums, even sitting in with his band on occasion—excellent physical and emotional therapy. With any fine motor skills that demanded digital dexterity I'd practice to proficiency.

In May of my senior year I hosted a graduation party for my entire class of 1978. Dad helped us get a keg of beer, which was a pretty standard parental approach for senior celebrations. He was loved by many of my peers and hung out with us for a while, serving guests despite the fact that he was making one of several attempts to get on the wagon. His tolerant attitude merely reflected that of most of my friends' parents, who accepted their kids' drinking as just part of growing up.

That summer I worked long hours insulating newly constructed homes, reserving the month before college to travel cross-country with Tweeter and Buddy. We backpacked from the Teton Range south through the Rocky Mountains, into the desert and Grand Canyon, as well as through many states between Ohio and eastern California. It was an enlightening adventure but also a time for poignant reflection on my choices in life and the convictions shaping my character.

My blurred vision regarding the effects of alcohol followed me to college despite my acute awareness of the damage it was causing to Dad and to those around him. Volunteer work in hospitals had reinforced my inspiration to help others faced with debilitating challenges. That fall I began pre–physical therapy studies at Ohio University (OU) in Athens, one of the state's most charming southern towns, which is tucked within the mountains bordering West Virginia.

My choice to begin college at OU was partly motivated by Tweeter's decision to join me. We had been approved to reside in Hoover House, the co-ed "honors tutorial" housing that consisted of higher achieving first-year and upper-level undergrads, as well as graduate students. This allowed us to be roommates while escaping the otherwise restrictive mandate that all freshmen reside separately from upper-class students. This way, at least physically, we were removed from the proximity of freshman dormitory housing and the associated temptations of a carefree party-zone atmosphere.

Still, I'd convinced myself that life was too short to miss an opportunity to celebrate, regardless of the cost. So I developed an effective although unconventional game plan: I would study hard during the week so that I could party hard over the weekend as a reward.

The physical therapy curriculum paralleled programs for students aiming at medical school admission. As I continued my undergraduate studies, I occasionally imagined a career as a physician. However, I knew from the many days I'd spent as a patient that the academic and lifestyle commitments demanded more than I was willing to give. My partying and social adventures would need to become few and far between, if not extinct altogether. Meanwhile, a career in physical therapy would be intellectually stimulating while allowing a measure of professional autonomy—and more one-on-one time with patients. Part-time employment in the University Health Center and its small PT department afforded me beneficial practical experience.

Nonetheless, the idea of becoming a doctor lodged itself in a corner of my mind like an ungerminated seed. With a modicum of attention to time management, I was able to stay on top of the strenuous demands of a scientific curriculum. Fortunately, I had tested out of the freshman English requirement, allowing me to supplement the dry studies of science with electives in literature and creative writing. I'd always been a voracious reader and tried to keep up with my journaling.

Upon returning to OU for my sophomore year, I resumed my residence in Hoover House, but sadly without Tweeter. Finances and family obligations made it impossible for him to come back for his second year. We had been comrades in arms throughout high school, often working part-time jobs together to pay for college tuition, so it was hard to see him have to choose employment in a manufacturing company over continued education. My best friend, who had been a pillar of strength during my time in the hospital and my roommate as we took our first steps into the big world away from home, would not be at my side. His day-to-day absence left a regrettable void.

Exiting the elevator at my floor soon after arriving back on campus, I caught a brief glimpse of an attractive blonde. Barefooted, tanned, and wearing a turquoise bathrobe, she was standing in the doorway of the RA (resident assistant) room finishing a conversation with another student.

I assumed that either my RA had a lovely girlfriend or I had a lovely RA. As I headed to my room, I crossed my fingers and hoped for the latter.

19

LEARNING

As I entered my assigned room for my sophomore year, I was greeted with a holler from my new roommate: "Hey there, brother McD. How's it goin'?" Greg Beach, aka "Beachola," and I were well acquainted from our freshman year. Getting to bunk with someone I knew well eased some of the sadness held over from losing Tweeter.

"Have you met the RA yet?" was Beachola's next question.

"No," I replied, "but I hope she's the lovely blonde gal who caught my attention in the doorway of the RA quarters."

He responded affirmatively.

"I need to introduce myself," I told him.

I didn't have to wait long. Shortly thereafter Katie appeared in the doorway of our room. With soft blonde shoulder-length curls and lightly tanned skin, she was dressed in jeans and a flannel shirt. She took in everything with a furtive scan followed by a brief locking of her eyes with mine. Hers were alluring and sparkled blue, in harmony with a warm, inviting smile. She radiated a beguiling charisma.

"Your roommate was telling me about you and it's so nice to finally meet!" she said to me. I was immediately smitten.

Naturally I was anxious to learn the details of her life. Katie was from New Jersey and was studying to be a special education teacher. There were at least a couple of strikes against my pursuing her: she was a senior while I was just starting my sophomore year, and she was already in a serious relationship. Her boyfriend had graduated from OU the previous year and was working in Cleveland, coming back to campus only occasionally to visit.

I was determined, however, and over the next few weeks I managed to engineer reasons to knock on Katie's door with a question or run into her on the catwalk to chat about anything I could think of. As the fall quarter wore on, I made small gestures that I hoped subtly revealed my affections. Truth be told, I was infatuated with her in a way I had never known.

I wasn't alone in my admiration. KTP, a diminutive I coined for Katie Poage (her first and middle names), had a natural interest in and genuine love for people that was only exceeded by her incredible love of life; most everyone she'd meet thrived on the opportunity to simply be around her.

We found that we had many interests in common, especially music. I thought my own musical affinities were widespread, but Katie blew me away. I had never met anyone with a greater knowledge of artists and their song lyrics. Her musical tastes ranged from the sixties and Woodstock, with artists like Joni Mitchell and Crosby, Stills, Nash & Young, to more current genres, including local talent and lesser-known musicians.

By the end of October, I had persuaded Katie to join me on a road trip to my family's favorite annual fall destination—Cook Forest, Pennsylvania. There were so many special memories associated with this place I'd returned to every year from the time when I was six or seven: the log cabins, the colors and smells of fall, the traditional game of capture the flag.

Katie's other relationship had run its course, and the eight-hour drive from Athens gave us some extended together time. It also provided an opportunity to drive the 1967 Dodge Coronet convertible with two-toned leather seats that I had lovingly restored with my grandfather during the summer. I had bought the car from Penny, who'd purchased it new upon her graduation from OU.

As Katie and I grew closer I began to learn a lot about myself while developing a more mature love, admiration, and respect for members of the opposite sex. Katie taught me many things about loving people and trusting others, soothing and easing some of the emotional scars from the fire. Having lost two people I loved dearly, I'd become cautious about committing to others. Katie helped me begin to know and appreciate unconditional love.

I stuck with my disciplined approach to studying, though both Katie and I enjoyed drinking beer on our off nights or over an occasional long weekend. I was always careful about controlling my drinking, having promised myself to never develop the habits that had hurt Dad and those around him. Frequently we'd visit Katie's older brother Bill in Dayton, Ohio. A multitalented musician, he'd host weekends of partying around his baby grand piano and four-track recorder. Playing guitars and singing was a welcome respite from academia.

The situation at home wasn't improving, however. Dad

made several attempts to cut back on his drinking. He even stopped entirely on his own for a time during the first couple of years after I left for school. But he always slipped back into his disease, the "normal" state for one in the throes of addiction. Eventually Penny gave him an ultimatum: if he continued drinking, she would cease making trips back to Cleveland from New York, and the romance that was blossoming between them would be over.

It took an intervention that included pleas from all of us to finally convince Dad to seek help in climbing out of the dark hole in which he was trapped. I went home to drive him to the renowned Rosary Hall addiction treatment center at St. Vincent Charity Hospital in Cleveland. Sister Mary Ignatia Gavin, also known as "the Angel of Alcoholics Anonymous," had founded the program in the early 1950s. She had previously worked in Akron, Ohio, where Dr. Bob Smith and Bill Wilson co-founded Alcoholics Anonymous in 1935. While there, Sister Ignatia arranged for a patient with an alcohol-induced gastritis to be admitted to the hospital for treatment, marking the first time alcoholism was approached as a medical problem. She also instituted the well-known tradition of handing out medallions to AA members to commemorate months or years of sobriety.

Through his time at Rosary Hall and with the help of his sponsor and others, Dad eventually remained sober. He continued life with a new freedom and formula for living through his ongoing involvement with AA.

As I studied at OU, I began thinking again about applying to medical school. I was feeling more secure about my ability to handle the science curriculum and started weighing the pros and cons of a career as a doctor compared with that of a physical therapist.

Regardless of my decision, I decided to transfer to Ohio State University (OSU), which had a physical therapy school and a medical school, enhancing my chances of acceptance to one or the other. There were additional factors prompting the move. The OSU campus in Columbus was where my brother Tim was enrolled and was only about an hour east of Sidney, Ohio, where Katie had taken a job after graduating with her bachelor's degree in K–12 special education.

The distance between Columbus and Sidney was certainly long compared with the proximity we had enjoyed living down the hall from one another at OU, but it was manageable.

The decision to stay with physical therapy was somewhat influenced by a medical intern living in an adjacent unit to mine. I may have seen him a total of six times throughout the whole year; he worked such demanding hours and I'd hear him leaving the house at 4:00 a.m. At best such a life appeared unbalanced.

My part-time work and volunteer experiences exposed me to the wide spectrum of clinical specialties where PTs focused their energies. Some of these included the hospital burn unit where I was a patient as well as Rainbow Babies and Children's Hospital, where I had recovered from GBS. Through these varied opportunities I could capitalize on the insights acquired surviving both a major burn injury with multiple reconstructive surgeries and a debilitating neurological disease, offering a professional perspective in addition to my unique personal knowledge.

Cleveland State University (CSU) was my first choice, even over OSU, among the schools to which I had applied. It would allow me to live in my hometown with Dad and Penny, where I'd save on expenses. Also, Cleveland held an excellent reputation for medical education and training, with three major universities and the prestigious Cleveland Clinic as well as Case Western Reserve University and its renowned medical school. There were also several state-of-the-art hospitals.

So, I completed the lengthy application and interview process. It was extremely competitive, with a limited number of spots available for the thousands of applicants. Katie and I were visiting her brother over spring break when I received a phone call from the dean of CSU's physical therapy school. I was ecstatic to hear that I was granted a position for the following year, contingent upon my completion of all the science prerequisites.

Dad's recovery initiated many changes in his relationships while the one with Penny deepened. The love that had been growing between the two of them flourished, and they were married at St. Angela Merici church in Fairview Park on August 23, 1980. We were all delighted about the union. The ceremony's celebrant, Father Jim Becherer, was a dear friend of the McDonough family, having met Mom and Dad at a Marriage Encounter seminar several years before the fire. Father Jim had also buried Mom and Toby and would preside over many more family passages, including weddings and funerals.

Beyond academic achievements there were still reconstructive procedures that I needed to undergo. Dr. Earle did

several surgeries on my face and neck to release contractures and scarring that had restricted my ability to rotate my
neck. Although there were no guarantees of success, in my
case excising the thick keloid scars improved my mobility
and appearance. Numerous hand surgeries followed, each
mandating lengthy post-op therapy. Progress seemed slow
in comparison to other facets of my life, but it was evident,
if often only one day at a time.

By the time I began PT school, the dexterity and function in both of my hands had been significantly restored.
I could play the piano again, a therapeutic hobby, and was
even ready to perform surgical dissection of human cadavers
in anatomy lab.

It took nearly three additional years to finish PT school,
an intensive period that entailed class and lab instruction
eight hours per day without a summer break. Full-time
coursework, academic and practical, was taught by some
of Cleveland's most reputable practitioners from all medical
specialties—including Dr. Fratianne. That year I accepted his
invitation to appear as a former patient of the burn unit, now
a student, in front of a classroom of 128 medical students he
was teaching. In that role I was asked to disrobe before the
entire class to "model" my scarred but healed body.

It often intrigued me that despite the more obvious scars
of my hands and upper extremities, other burn survivors
frequently did not notice them at first. I realized that patients in acute distress are focused on their own condition
almost exclusively. Only later, as their physical condition
improves, do they begin to notice things outside their
immediate sphere—such as the burn scars of their own
therapist.

This aha moment became a reliable barometer for marking their psychological recovery and a time when they seemed most receptive to emotional support and encouragement. I was often inspired to capitalize on a patient's ability to identify with my circumstances, allowing our shared struggles to fortify their emotional strength and endurance.

While I was doing an internship at the Shriner Burns Institute in Cincinnati, I worked with a patient who had very bad burns to his hands. He was an auto mechanic who had been trying to pour gasoline into the carburetor of a car when it exploded. I showed him photographs of how my hands had been and then let him see how they looked after reconstructive surgeries. It was rewarding to find specific activities to improve his dexterity and range of motion.

As part of another internship in neurological rehabilitation through Florida Hospital in Orlando, I visited the burn unit at the nearby Orlando Regional Medical Center. I was beginning to appreciate that some of my most challenging yet emotionally enriching opportunities included work with burn injury and trauma survivors who taught me that I had something unique to offer them—hope. It was deeply humbling.

During the summer after graduation I passed my boards and began interviewing for positions in rehabilitation departments of large teaching and university-affiliated hospitals. For me, the primary prerequisite for each potential institution was the presence of an actively progressive burn unit that employed PTs as vital members of the burn team.

After five years of dating Katie, our paths were beginning to diverge. Although we still loved and respected each other, individually we had career interests and goals that demanded relatively greater priority than those necessary for building and maintaining a relationship—at least romantically.

Neither of us was ready at that time in our professional lives to invest the necessary elements required of a long-term relationship. We slowly drifted apart, with neither of us finding it necessary to analyze the reasons why. Perhaps our individual career paths had greater allure than the path we were following together. Fortunately, we continued to love and respect each other and value our friendship.

One lazy afternoon I was sitting at home mulling over the merits of the hospitals at which I'd interviewed. The phone rang: on the line was Bob Kogut, Director of Rehabilitation at the Orlando Regional Medical Center (ORMC). He told me he was reviewing a copy of my CV that I had left when visiting their burn unit during my neurological internship at a neighboring Florida hospital.

As we talked it quickly became evident that he and I had many common interests and ideals, including music. In fact, with the instant familiarity we seemed to share, it felt as though we'd known each other for years. An hour later, I accepted a position in the department as one of ten staff therapists. A week later I began practice as a PT in the burn unit, among other specialty areas.

Through our shared affinity for music, Bob and I forged a close friendship beyond our professional bond as therapists as he taught me new guitar skills. He was a talented fiddle player and introduced me to bluegrass music, inviting me to jam regularly with some of the most colorful characters in the south—even once with the famous Bill Monroe.

20

SAILING

The sound of the approaching helicopter sparked an adrenaline surge, reminding me of the downwind rush felt rounding the final mark in a sailing regatta. Everything in me poised to dive into action, the momentum fueled by excitement.

As we waited in the burn unit at ORMC, we would hear the *whup-whup-whup* of the blades on the air ambulance that would hover pendulously before settling on the rooftop helipad.

Sharing 24/7 on-call duties with a colleague, I would be paged to the unit whenever a serious case came in. We were one of four regional burn units in the state, and the burn-injured patients were victims of house fires, industrial explosions, motor vehicle accidents, or careless mishaps such as pouring gas onto a charcoal fire.

Then there were the child abuse cases—babies, infants, and older children with hot-iron burns on their backsides or with the telltale "stocking feet" pattern, evidence of having been dipped in scalding water.

ORMC was somewhat atypical in terms of utilizing PTs as part of the first response team in the burn unit. In many other hospitals, rehabilitation was separate from wound care and began only after the patient had been assessed and stabilized. But involvement from the time of admission allowed for a more comprehensive team approach to care.

As the PT, I was responsible for evaluating the extent and depth of a patient's burns while one of the resident physicians addressed the ABCs of trauma: airway, breathing, and circulation. While the resident and nurses intubated the patient and gained IV access, I'd document on the Lund-Browder form the total body percentage and depth of the burns so that appropriate fluid resuscitation could begin.

Once the patient was physiologically stable, an assistant and I would transport them on a specialized gurney to the tank room, much like the one in which I had been treated only eight years earlier. With a nurse on hand to assist with procedures and administer IV medications, we would cleanse the burns, debride loose tissue, and evaluate range of motion before dressing the burns with topical creams. Beyond the initial assessment, the tank room routine would be a daily occurrence coordinated with staff, allowing me to fabricate splints and facilitate specific therapeutic exercises to prevent contractures. It also allowed me to work closely with the residents and attending surgeons.

In many burn units dressing changes were exclusively nursing responsibilities, whereas in ours these duties were shared by nurses and physical therapists. This proved advantageous for many reasons, including better continuity of care among the providers and, most importantly, more accurate evaluation of range of motion and wound or graft healing by the entire burn team.

Occasionally I would go to the operating room to fabricate splints for application following surgery and to better assess passive range of motion while the patient was anesthetized and thus pain-free. Working closely with the surgeons stimulated and inspired my interest in surgery while also improving my knowledge base. It further enhanced my ability to reinforce the doctors' instructions and teaching to the patients.

After some time, I began to appreciate that burn care providers often fell onto a spectrum between lenient and empathetic at one end, and firm or forceful at the other. In other words, some caregivers were more inclined to give the patient a needed break whereas others were likely to push and encourage them to the extreme of their limits. Ideally, the best staff could shift from one extreme to the other as the situation required.

My experience as a burn patient made it easier for me so that I fell somewhere in the middle. I could understand patients feeling belligerent or resistant, but I also knew I needed to find ways to motivate, encourage, and support them through tasks they'd otherwise refuse.

I'd never say to a patient, "I know what you're feeling." When appropriate or if asked, I'd find ways to share my own experience, thereby revealing my ability to *understand* what they were feeling. Many days this proved to be an artful psychological challenge more easily said than done. Sometimes I couldn't help but fantasize about having the tools necessary to effect a greater difference in burn care. At the very least this would require going to medical school. Usually these thoughts passed quickly, overshadowed by my fear that I didn't have the discipline to pursue such lofty aspirations. *Do I? And besides, would there be time left in a day for life?*

Working with burn patients was most gratifying for me, though I also enjoyed practice in orthopedics, wound care, pain management, and spinal cord injury, as well as neurology and stroke rehabilitation. After several years in a large teaching hospital, I was presented with an opportunity to become an associate in a private practice. This gave me further experience with the business side of health care along with contracting and providing rehabilitation services to area nursing homes.

Meanwhile, much of my free time was spent on the water: what had been an occasional pastime became a consuming passion when I moved to Orlando. Having learned to sail on Lake Erie when I was a boy, I had always enjoyed all types of boating, but especially sailing.

From training to earn my pilot license during undergraduate years at OU, I knew that the physics of flying and sailing were similar. Wind creates a negative pressure on the skyward side of a wing or the windward side of a sail—the rest amounts to steering a desired course. Eventually, I bought and customized a trailerable sloop that I enjoyed sailing all over Florida's many lakes and miles of coastline.

I had to be protective of my hands, however. A long weekend grappling with lines and sails would leave them sore and slightly swollen. I had to make sure to wear gloves to protect the skin, particularly in the grafted areas, which was prone to breaking down if taxed too hard.

Sailing was also a good metaphor for my life. Having left the safe harbor of home, I had set out in uncharted waters, eager to explore what lay ahead. There were some stormy seas, but I felt confident of my ability to navigate them. And there were plenty of days of sunshine and delight. What I didn't realize was that part of my inner compass was failing, and I was slowly drifting more and more off course.

If you had asked me whether I trusted God to guide and protect me, I would probably have answered an emphatic yes. My faith was strong, or so I believed. After all, I had seen the proverbial burning bush during my near-death experience. God's existence was no longer in question for me; I knew it with certainty. But, partly as a side effect of what I had experienced, I had been subtly cultivating a negative trait that resulted in an inflated sense of power or autonomy. I eventually came to realize what a struggle it was keeping a connection between what I knew to be true intellectually with what I wanted to feel in my heart spiritually.

I shared the strong need for independence common to children of alcoholics. Establishing and maintaining my independence had become second nature. This drive to be in control began to impair my ability to trust others, including God. Over time, I gradually grew fearful of asking anyone, and more importantly God, for help.

I still prayed quite regularly, typically along the lines of, "God, I'm so grateful to have you in my life; you're so powerful and amazing!" But the idea of giving him ultimate authority in all areas of my life was a foreign concept.

The carefree lifestyle associated with sailing went drink-in-hand with partying. There was always plenty of cold beer or the fixings for margaritas close by during three- and four-day breaks on the water. Gradually, I began drinking more in quantity and in frequency. As I did I became less focused on the direction of my career and its associated goals. I began living for the weekends, with freedom from responsibility a priority. Soon the "weekends" were starting on Thursday and ending on Monday morning, leaving me in want of a hair of the dog pick-me-up. The various ports of call I made became something of a blur; many times it was a wonder that I made it home without a serious mishap.

Somewhere in my mind, I knew my drinking was becoming habitual, if not problematic. Despite having told myself I'd never develop a drinking problem like Dad, I was falling into the ways of addiction. In addition, I was managing my finances with much less discipline, acquiring a fair amount of debt. Living on credit cards was becoming routine, as was my casual, cavalier disregard for paying extreme interest rates. I was earning good money but driving around in a six-year-old Chevy van because I couldn't afford to replace it.

My ship was slowly sinking and I'd yet to notice the leak.

Although not clinically depressed, in a general sense I was becoming relatively more and more unhappy. Life began to lose some of the magical appeal that once seemed so evident. And the drinking blackouts that I'd experienced occasionally back in my early college years were now occurring more frequently. This was concerning during the occasional times when I was able to reflect honestly on my circumstances: I knew that experiencing blackouts, forgetting the details of an evening or day, was a clear and specific symptom of alcoholism.

Most troubling was the recognition that, spiritually, I was now lost at sea, blindly passing through dense fog without the guidance of a lighthouse. Increasingly, guilt was smothering the inner light that had warmed the cooler places in my heart since the awakening I'd enjoyed through my near-death experience. Deep down I felt I was living a less-than-authentic life.

Living on an idyllic piece of Florida real estate with nearly two hundred feet of lakefront, I had a great location for what became a celebrated annual Lake Bash Blowout. The daylong event featured sailing, waterskiing, jet skiing, volleyball—and drinking. I hosted a large crowd of friends, doctors, and therapists who enjoyed a barbecue and clambake, a huge fire pit, and kegs of beer, all while soaking up the sun.

After one such party, my roommate's friend Kathy began taking an interest in me that I had no business entertaining. The fact that I did says more than a little regarding the state of my mental acuity and decline on the alcohol abuse spectrum. It doesn't say much for her ability to judge the book within the cover either. Anyway, we foolishly decided to take a weekend trip to Bonita Springs on the Gulf, which resulted in a near-fatal crash on I-75 when I rolled her Mustang into the northbound lane after being cut off by some kids who never even stopped.

The alcohol-fueled accident was definitely a wake-up call. I knew that the financial and physical consequences could have been much worse. As the shock wore off and the bruising started to fade, I prayed for forgiveness and asked God to help me bring some order back to my life.

A couple weeks later, my friend Bob, who had originally hired me at ORMC, pulled me aside at Winter Park Memorial Hospital, where I was now working as a private contractor PT. He was now the director of rehabilitation there, having also left ORMC. We had become good friends since he first recruited me for the burn unit position. Though he was not my direct boss at Winter Park, he was responsible for the contracted professionals providing services for his department.

"Hey, Mark," he said. "Somebody mentioned that your breath smelled like alcohol when you were with them." There was a question in his statement. "You've been out partying too late. You know, if there's a problem, you need to nip it in the bud. And I would support you in any way I can."

Bob's kind caution got through to me, and for the second time since our initial phone meeting, he prompted me toward a formative life choice. His words stuck with me over the next couple of days as I played through the past months in my head. If I was honest with myself, I knew that I didn't need to be jobless, living under a bridge and clutching a bottle of liquor, to have a drinking problem. I was a daily drinker, physically dependent.

From Dad's involvement with AA, I knew who I needed to call. I knew that the first step out of this stranglehold was to "admit powerlessness over alcohol." Clearly, my life had become unmanageable. And I also knew that to admit defeat was to accept a life without alcohol, so I asked myself, *If I write this check, is it one that I can cash?*

I'd yet to realize that sometimes surrendering can lead to a victory. After hours of mental wrestling, at about 3:30 a.m. on Wednesday, October 1, 1986, I woke Dad with a phone call from my couch in Orlando.

"Dad," I told him, "I have a problem with alcohol; I think I'm an alcoholic."

"Thank God," he said, offering the loving, calm words I needed to hear. "Don't worry, son, it's going to be okay—so much more than okay."

21

SOBER

Asking for and then receiving Dad's support regarding my decision to get sober was additional inspiration motivating me to remain committed toward change. I didn't want to disappoint him, and now I had accountability. His encouragement meant so much; now that I had it, there was no turning back.

Shortly after I hung up, Dan called. He had found a similar path into recovery a few years ahead of me. Soon after following me to OU, he allowed partying to become a priority and ran in the same social circles and fraternities as I did.

I felt a twinge of shame knowing that I needed life advice from him when I should have been the responsible older brother. I paced back and forth in my kitchen as we spoke, trying to determine what kind of detoxification program I needed: controlled or monitored. I was especially nervous since I hadn't had a drink for a while, causing me to feel apprehension and a simultaneous sense of relief. I confessed to Dan that I was really scared, if not terrified.

"Keep asking God to give you the strength to not drink, just for today," he said. "And Mark, it *will* get better, so much better, I promise you."

Those last few words rang loud and clear, even if everything else I'd heard seemed a blur. They rang crisp with a truth spoken from personal experience. I was moved to realize my younger brother had my back.

I told my roommate, Tim, about my decision, and he called his mother, an addictions counselor. To ensure anonymity, she recommended a city-run facility, which happened to be for indigent men who had no money or insurance, allowing them to detoxify from alcohol for three days. She arranged for me to be admitted to an inner-city detox tank run by MACO (Metropolitan Alcohol Council of Orlando).

It seemed I'd waited several hours before getting checked into the facility. Eventually, somewhere near 9:00 p.m., a large woman introduced herself as Yvonne. She had intense black eyes closely set in a round face. She was not quite obese, but her sizable frame and weight made her appear as big as a house to me. As she extracted a basic history, I made a point to tell her that I would need heavy sedation in order to sleep.

"I've had many pain medications and sedatives over the years due to my reconstructive surgeries," I told her with a confident, slightly insolent tone. "And I'm going to need a lot of something strong to knock me out."

Without missing a beat Yvonne retorted, "Now you listen here, child. I've been doing this for as long as you've been living! Don't you be thinking you're gonna tell me how to do my job, or else you'll see just how many ways I *can* knock you out!

You've been hitting the bottle too hard and too long; don't be telling me nothing. Now you just take this and get your pretty backside in here on one of those cots and get to sleep."

With that she handed me one Librium pill in a white paper cup and directed me to a room full of steel cots. As I walked into the dimly lit room I felt a chill run through my arms and torso. The room was damp and dreary, with unadorned cinder-block walls. At the far end on the left was a window draped with a black shade. Three or four bodies occupying several cots appeared to be asleep.

Timidly I chose a cot near the doorway, as I was afraid to venture any farther into the unfamiliar room. Like the other cots it was made from a steel frame to which a trampoline-style vinyl canvas was attached by small individual springs. The mattress was no more than a scant rubber pad on which was folded a thin white blanket.

Feeling rather fainthearted and alone, I knelt on the cold cement floor beside the empty cot. Then I prayed.

"Oh God, if ever there was a time I needed you—and there have been many—I sure do need you now."

I told him how fearful I was. How I knew that, whatever God's will, it was not for me to continue drinking and partying my days away. Knowing I could do nothing alone, I asked the Holy Spirit to please relieve me and guide me.

Part of the reason for my apprehension was the knowledge that for the preceding year, I had never gone to sleep without being partially inebriated. In fact, sometimes waking in the middle of the night mandated a shot or two to resume slumber.

"God," I prayed, "I think I'm doing the right thing; please be with me."

As I lay down on the cot, I could feel deeply suppressed emotions of shame rising to the surface. A lump formed in my throat, and as tears filled my eyes, objects in the room took on a glassy appearance. I swiped at my wet cheeks with my shirtsleeve.

My next conscious moment was at 8:00 a.m. the following day. I awoke having slept through the night as soundly as a hibernating bear. I could hardly believe it.

I was certain that the relief washing over me was the mercy of God, a gift I was overjoyed to receive. Miraculously, it had been only twenty-four hours since I had admitted to having a problem and voluntarily agreed to detoxification. By doing so, I had committed to a completely new way of living, and I was overwhelmed with joy and a sense of exhilaration.

I still felt a bit skittish, but I was surprisingly energized about a new and fresh potential to become a man of convictions instead of a counterfeit of intentions. God had begun some form of a spiritual transformation in me. I'd learn later that it was the instant kind of spiritual experience as opposed to those of the slower educational variety.

One of the guys on a nearby cot looked half asleep and disheveled. With a raspy voice he said, "So you're one of the newbies who came in last night?" He went on to explain that everyone had to get in the medication line at the nurse's office and then get breakfast before the AA meeting started in a half hour. Then he told me that this was his seventh or eighth time in the unit in as many months.

I followed my new roommate to the medication line, where eight or ten other guys were waiting to receive whatever meds had been ordered for them. I felt like I'd gone to sleep and awakened in the psychiatric ward from *One Flew Over the Cuckoo's Nest*. Some of the guys looked like they had been living in a dumpster, and a few probably had.

Reaching the dispensing point, I noticed that Yvonne the battle-ax had gone home and been replaced by a younger version. This nurse handed me some vitamins and something to help with the withdrawal symptoms. She seemed surprised that I appeared so calm and collected, explaining that my admission records indicated I'd been somewhat distraught the night before. I told her it was a miracle that I'd slept through the night.

At 8:30 a.m. we all convened in the meeting room, where some "former inmates" from the community chaired an AA meeting. After opening the proceedings, John, the chairman, asked that we identify ourselves one at a time by first name.

Most of the guys stated their names and said they were alcoholics. When it was my turn I said, "Hi, my name is Mark, and I'm an alcoholic." It was the first time I'd openly admitted it, despite telling Dad that I suspected as much. Speaking the words felt as though the weight of the world had been lifted from my shoulders, and my eyes gradually filled with tears as the introductions continued around the room.

In my teens I had been to several open AA meetings with my father, where friends or family members could attend as guests. I had also been to Al-Anon meetings for the loved ones of alcoholics, so I had some understanding of the twelve-step program. But since dropping to my knees and praying, everything seemed different. The life I was saving was my own. Perhaps I realized some sense of humility, and God opened my eyes to see things clearly for the first time in a long time.

The first step was to admit I was an alcoholic and that life had become unmanageable, a word that refers to a series of recurring mishaps that could have been avoided if not for the effects of habitual alcohol abuse. That described my life perfectly.

The second step talks about believing "that a power greater than ourselves could restore us to sanity." The third step says, "We made a decision to turn our will and our lives over to the care of God as we understood him." Check and check; I clearly fit the bill here as well. In fact, much of the disorder in my life was the result of self-will and my fear of allowing God to remain in charge.

I had no difficulty believing in him, especially since my near-death experience ten years earlier. But my personal relationship with God had deteriorated to the point where, though I remained grateful for his presence in my life, I was making decisions based only on self. I had ceased relying upon him to guide or steer me.

After three days of meetings and therapy sessions, I was given a schedule for AA meetings in Orange County and sent home. I still had the physical symptoms of being newly detoxed: jittery, with shaking and mild trembling in my hands. But I was getting better each day. My friend Bob welcomed me back as a contracting therapist two days later. That day I instituted a new routine that involved attending a meeting at some point in my daily schedule. The frequent availability of meetings close to where I lived and worked made this convenient.

The Greenhouse, in downtown Winter Park, was a vacant house where AA meetings were held several times daily and in the evenings. Among the faces I saw there were leading members of the local business and civic community. Recalling the men I had just spent three days with in the detox unit, I was reminded that alcoholism knows no social barriers or limits.

L ike many people embracing a sober lifestyle, I had been advised to do "ninety in ninety"—attend ninety meetings in my first ninety days of sobriety—as a tool for establishing a strong foundation in recovery.

The AA meeting schedule for Orlando listed hundreds of meetings at various times, seven days a week. This made daily attendance easy; I usually went to one early in the day or at noon, and again in early or late evening.

I was floating on a bit of a "pink cloud," as old-timers in the recovery world describe the early days of drink-free clarity. I was definitely excited about my new sober way of life and determined to continue living one day at a time in my new spiritually and physically energized state. Time would be the true test of my resolve.

Through AA I began to understand more about how the disease of alcoholism had affected my family and me. Evidence points to a genetic cause for the disease, with an equal propensity among males and females. Although I had become increasingly aware of my father's struggle with alcoholism in my teens and twenties, I had told myself I would never allow my own drinking to become similarly problematic.

It was no great leap for me to see how some of Dad's drinking to excess had been an understandable reaction to immense anguish and to such crushing tragedy. He still often thought of those smoke detectors that had been awaiting installation. I also came to realize how, years later, some of my misuse of alcohol and drugs was partly a means of coping with my own pain.

Initially I believed that drinking a few beers was truly for medicinal purposes and therapeutically it did help alleviate much of the physical pain related to my scarring and contractures. But ultimately drinking became a problem that made my life unmanageable. It also negatively affected my spiritual connection with God as well as my personal and professional relationships.

One of the most affirming and sweetest milestones in my early sobriety came a couple months after I walked out of the detox unit. I returned to Fairview Park to visit my father, seeing him in person for the first time since that late-night phone call.

While I was there he presented me with a copy of *The Big Book*, the standard AA textbook. Inside the cover he wrote this inscription:

Mark: Contained herein is a message of hope and a formula for truth. If you continue to truly try to understand the message and live by the formula, you have a promise of true happiness. This will happen not only from a drug-free life experience, but also from a resultant realization of progressive joy.

Love, Dad
11/13/86

22

DESPERATION

Those who achieve sobriety often do so by receiving the gift of desperation as their last resort—though it's usually in hindsight that it's recognized as a gift. In my case I was thoroughly tired of alcohol and its consequences in my life, and I was willing to do anything. I was sick and tired of being sick and tired, as the saying goes.

At the risk of sounding overly laudable, through sobriety I began to fully appreciate the need to realize my potential, becoming a man of my convictions. As it does for many, my recovery necessitated honesty, open-mindedness, and willingness. Personally, I also needed faith, integrity, and perseverance.

Those in the know suggest that it's best to avoid making any big life changes during the first year of sobriety, including places of residence, jobs, or new relationships. In reality, people rarely heed this advice, and I was no exception—ignoring all three recommendations.

Now sober, I sold my boat and moved out of my lakefront party house into one on the other side of Orlando. I also made the decision to form Intrinsic Rehabilitative Associates, PA. My new company provided contract services including PT, OT, and speech therapy to hospitals, clinics, and nursing homes throughout central Florida. As if that wasn't enough change, I also ended the codependent relationship in which I'd been taken hostage.

Living sober, my interpersonal relationships with friends and colleagues improved while new ones were cultivated. As expected, with the growth and changes in me, some of my old friendships either evolved or faded away.

Most importantly, my spiritual alliance with God took its rightful position in the center of my life. I began to consider and pray about new opportunities and directions. My faith also began to grow stronger as I learned to let God take control and strived to synchronize my plans with his will. I didn't know what the future held, but I sure knew who held it.

Being sober afforded me a new level of awareness. It was disheartening to realize how many hours I had wasted idly while telling myself that I deserved time to party or to celebrate one cause or another. In college and PT school, I had been able to remain disciplined where my studying skills were concerned. Now in sobriety I found more time for continuing education, exploring new practice ideas, and working with others.

More focused on character assets, I tried living more consistently by the moral code that shaped my belief system. Gradually, when I looked in the mirror, I began liking the person I saw there.

It became increasingly clear that my positive reality stemmed from confronting the tragedy in my life. Perhaps it was all part of God's intricate but complex plan, I reflected. Had the fire and my burn injury never happened, I'd have never become a physical therapist or been inspired by medicine and surgery. Instead I would have pursued a career in journalism or writing.

Without the acceptance of my alcoholism and God's grace to find recovery, I'd never have had the discipline or fortitude required to pursue further education, and I began to wonder if perhaps it was not too late to become a doctor. In my morning prayers, I asked God to show me a sign if this was his will for me. On Sundays I'd take my pet parrot, Rico, and head for New Smyrna Beach on the eastern coast, continually asking God to show me a sign if indeed it was his will that I seek admission to medical school.

For at least six weeks of Sundays, Rico and I continued our excursions to the beach, where I prayed and watched for some kind of sign. Arriving home late one afternoon, I was listening to a cassette tape of AA testimonies given to me by a friend. One of the speakers revealed how sobriety was the motivating factor that inspired him to gain admission to veterinary school at age thirty-five. I realized that if I abandoned this germination of a dream, I'd go on living life wondering *What if . . . ?* And at that point I knew in my heart that my decision had been made. It was exactly the sign I had prayed for.

"God," I said, "thank you. I'll begin this process one step at a time, and if any step is not your will, close the door."

Later that evening, I sat at my desk with a yellow legal pad in hand. I was reminded of an evening almost one year earlier when I successfully outlined and fulfilled a twelve-step plan to get to a Phil Collins concert. The first step was to put gas into my van and the last step involved snaking my way to the front row. It was a special sober memory.

After a brief prayer for guidance, I now listed a twelve-step plan for the next chapter on my journey. The last step read "Open acceptance letter to medical school."

I knew that to meet the premed requirements I'd need a year or more of college studies, including organic chemistry, calculus, cellular biology, and most likely a higher level of physics than the one I had completed for admission to PT school. Though my undergraduate major was in zoology, it had been nearly five years since I'd been a student, and the extra science classes with labs would be needed to strengthen my application. Thus, I needed to find local universities offering the required courses while ensuring they were transferable.

In addition, I had to finish the courses with A grades to be academically competitive. Finally, I'd need to complete a review course for the Medical College Admissions Test (MCAT), register for and successfully pass the test, and then complete the extensive application process to medical schools.

The preliminary paperwork alone was overwhelming. Moreover, tuition and the cost of living required that I continue working a minimum of thirty to forty hours per week while achieving the other prerequisites. The preparation could take three or more years—assuming I was successful with each step along the way. And that was even before the final phase of applying to medical schools. The entire process would mean committing to many more years.

Realistically, I could be thirty by the time I began medical school and forty or older by the time I established an independent practice. Then again, I acknowledged that if I nixed the idea altogether, I'd still wake up at age forty wondering what might have happened had I taken the first step toward such a goal.

Meanwhile, my new sober life allowed the renewing, repairing, and further healing of family relationships, improving connections with my father and my brothers. The McDonough boys who had been dressed alike and walked in lockstep as kids were pursuing their own journeys along paths individualized by the dramatic turns resulting from the trauma of the fire.

Tim had attended OSU for a year but then took time away from his studies to pursue musical ambitions. He packed his drums into his old Skylark and hit the road for California. He and his bandmates realized some minor successes, including a jam with Joe Walsh, though ultimately he achieved greater heights selling cars than as a musician.

More educationally inclined, Dan had developed a renewed motivation for business pursuits after abandoning the party lifestyle. With an MBA and a Realtor's license, he was inspired toward various entrepreneurial ventures. Self-motivated to near obsession, Dan rarely did anything less than thoroughly. He was a natural capitalist and financial innovator.

My own physical and medical challenges aside, of the four sons who survived the fire, Packy struggled the most in coming to terms with August 3, 1976. To lose a mother at such a young age would be a crushing blow for any child. The void left from losing his close younger brother compounded the grief.

Some of the vigor and energy for which he had been known was gone. While always turned inward, he became more withdrawn and introverted, often choosing to be a loner—so characteristic of that "lost child" in a dysfunctional family. He kept some close friends, but even they could see a difference from the once-vibrant Packy. Before the flames, he always had a sparkle in his eyes and a subtle grin on the upturned corners of his mouth. Afterward, neither was commonly evident.

Packy and I grew closer through the exchange of letters that began while I was a freshman at OU. He had experimented with alcohol and pot with some of his friends during the teen years. Later he enrolled at OU like his brothers but then withdrew at the end of his first year as he began losing focus and had a below-average performance. Living at home, Packy was neither engaged in classes nor punching a clock. He soon developed a pattern of late-night adventures with buddies followed by sleeping late.

Dad made several attempts to motivate his youngest surviving son, encouraging him to live more constructively. But house rules for continuing to live at home as adults included that we either worked full-time, enrolled in college, or both. If we were carrying a full course load, Dad would provide financial assistance as long as we remained in good academic standing. But we were expected to work when possible—at least while on break—to supplement tuition costs.

Now sober, Dad was simply unable to condone Packy's continued lack of responsibility. He gave him an ultimatum that resulted in his moving to Texas to live with some peers and an ex-girlfriend from his days at Culver Academy, the boarding and military school he attended as a teen and where he seemed to have made great strides.

In Austin, Packy was accepted at a technical institute with the goal of becoming a paramedic. He and I kept in touch through the letters that began during my undergraduate years and continued sporadically while I was in PT school. My impression was that he wanted to get his life in more order before reestablishing his relationship with Dad. Despite Dad's efforts to keep open lines of communication between them, there was enough animosity to keep them closed.

One of the many things Packy and I discussed was how he'd witnessed his Culver Academy roommate commit suicide by jumping from a fourth-story window. Spiritually, Packy told me how he was opposed to suicide and that he felt a sense of rejection by and resentment toward this close friend.

Writing back, I shared my newfound sobriety with him and how I'd learned that long-standing resentments had kept me from achieving genuine happiness. I told him, in the same way that Dad had told me, how taking a personal moral inventory while releasing old resentments could restore fractured relationships.

At OU Packy spent plenty of hours partying, a pattern I felt certain persisted, at least sporadically, in Austin. I did not feel comfortable suggesting that he might have a problem with alcohol or drugs, though based on our family history I had some suspicions that he did. I could only pray that by sharing some of my awarenesses, perhaps I might effect a change in him by example, or at least motivate him toward some self-assessment.

Gathered as a family in Cleveland for Christmas in 1986, we all waited hopefully for notice from Packy that he'd be joining us for the holidays. There was no such word. Every time the wind blew on Christmas Day the side door would rattle, teasing Dad and us with the possibility that it might be Packy returning home. It never was. Dad was clearly upset but held his emotions close, not wanting to draw attention to the (missing) elephant in the middle of the otherwise festive family room.

Some months later, in the spring, I received a rather upbeat letter from Packy. He was excited to know that I was interested in medicine. He was even more elated to reveal that he'd graduate in the summer quarter from paramedic school, where he was third in his class.

He sounded so upbeat and positive. I could not have been prouder of his accomplishments, and I knew that Dad would be too. But Packy also felt strongly that he didn't want to reconnect with us all until after graduation. He was busily focused on his upcoming final exams and wanted to wait to share peremptory proof—documentation of his success.

After such an encouraging update, it was a shock when Bob Kogut pulled me aside at work on July 26, 1987. Once again, my friend was charged with a task I'd never wish on anyone. He came to me with news from Dad, who had answered the door at our home on North Park Drive that morning to a Fairview Park police officer.

"Mr. McDonough, I'm very sorry to inform you that your son, Patrick Hardman McDonough, was found dead early this morning in Austin, Texas," the officer had announced. Packy had been discovered by a first-floor tenant of his apartment building, hanging from his own second-floor balcony.

Wanting me to be informed in person by a close friend, Dad had called Bob and asked him to break the shocking news to me. I was bereft, heartbroken, and unable to speak. Beyond my own pain, though, I could not begin to imagine that of my poor father, and brothers too, once again blindsided by tragedy. I left for Cleveland on the next available flight, desolate with grief. Seeing all the normal, happy faces boarding the plane, it took all of my will to keep the floodgates closed, holding back the tears in which I'd otherwise drown. In the midst of crushing anguish, it's hard to accept that life continues normally for many people all around us.

The viewing and funeral services held over the subsequent days were a testament to the enduring love and empathy our community held for the McDonough family. Both days of visitation at Corrigan Funeral Home were extended beyond the usual six hours and included reception lines with unending trails of supportive friends.

At one point in the evening I stepped out of the reception line to use the bathroom. Inside, I witnessed Dad step away from rinsing his face at the sink only to break down in convulsive tears, weeping over the loss of so very much. The only thing I could do was hold him as we cried together.

The following day, just over a week after he had turned twenty-one, Packy was buried next to our loving mother and dear brother. The procession of cars out to the cemetery was reminiscent of the services for Mom and Toby eleven years earlier, with such an outpouring of heartfelt affection by friends and relatives. We were a family tried with much tragedy but also blessed with priceless and loving pillars of strength from so many.

Compounding the heartache of our loss was our bafflement at the manner. From what he had told me, I knew that Packy could not have chosen to take his own life if he had been in his right mind. We talked with the police officers who were investigating, but little information was forthcoming. There seemed to be something not quite right about the whole thing, a suggestion of inconsistency regarding details of the night he died. But whether Packy had been involved in some kind of stunt gone wrong or there was something more sinister underway that night, we were never able to determine.

Though Packy's death was a devastating blow, I busied myself, suppressing the anguish by focusing on the steps I had outlined toward admission to medical school. The more active I remained, the more stable I stayed emotionally.

The first step began with an advanced class in calculus at Leesburg Community College, where one of my old friends, Danny C. from Ohio University, was a teaching professor. Subsequent steps included admission to Rollins College in Winter Park and enrollment in three different science lab courses. Remaining steps would include letters of reference, the MCAT exam, and multiple applications—hopefully followed by interviews.

Meanwhile, I continued practicing PT, where maintaining flexible hours with my own company allowed me to be in class during the day so that I could see patients in the afternoons and evenings. Life quickly got much more hectic than I'd ever imagined. Between recovery meetings, college studies, studying for the MCAT, and work as a PT, some days I felt overextended.

I wondered if I'd bitten off more than I could chew in my first year of sobriety. My AA sponsor, Sigurd, received regular calls at all hours of the day and night as I ranted about losing my sanity. He reminded me that I was getting what I'd prayed for, but as always, he was encouraging and supportive. Never at a loss for enlightening pieces of wisdom or the appropriate prod to keep my ego in check, he characterized me as Don Quixote tilting at windmills.

I had plenty on my mind with work and studies, which limited time for social activities. But two young women I had seen more than once at meetings turned my head. They were sisters, nearly mirror images of one another except that one was blonde and the other brunette.

It was not just their looks that made them memorable. I'd recognized them as the daughters of a charming lady who also frequented meetings at the Greenhouse. Remarkably, her name was Penny, like my stepmother, and her physical attributes were amazingly similar to my own mother.

The resemblance was not something I alone noticed. Several months after I first met this older lady, my brother Dan was visiting from Cleveland and accompanied me to a meeting at the Greenhouse when she was in attendance. Upon seeing her, Dan had to momentarily leave the room in utter shock. Were it not for her southern accent, he was certain that our mother had been reincarnated as a recovering alcoholic in Winter Park, Florida.

On March 11, 1988, I went to a noon meeting, after which I introduced myself and began chatting with Kitty, the blonde daughter of Penny. Standing in the parking lot at the Greenhouse, she asked if I'd be going to a local dance planned for the upcoming weekend. I wasn't sure at that stage, so we casually swapped numbers as acquaintances would.

Following our chat, I met my good friend John at the Sunset Grill for lunch. He had been sober for about eighteen months like I had. We sat across from each other at a four-top table, making small talk. As we did, he nodded hello to someone walking behind me.

Always the gentleman, John said, "Mark, I'd like you to meet a friend of mine, Joan."

I turned to make the acquaintance.

It was Kitty's brunette sister—and the reason I remember the date.

23

ROMANCE

As I stood and turned to shake hands with John's friend, I found myself drawn into a pair of deep amber eyes that shone over a warm smile and soft facial features. Joan Galbraith was instantly striking in a kelly-green suit with a crisp white blouse fastened at her subtle olive neckline by an onyx brooch. She offered a warm, firm handshake, exuding a confident and comfortable southern charm.

Usually at ease and quick to engage new people in conversation, for once I found myself struggling to string together a coherent greeting. Joan did not seem fazed. After expressing her pleasure at making my acquaintance, she sauntered with a surefooted gait to a table by the window, where she was obviously dining with business associates. I just stood there flustered until John's hearty laugh startled me back to the present and I settled back into my seat.

"Wow, John, I just met her sister Kitty at the noon meeting," I said. "But I've got to get to know Joan too!"

"No you don't," John shot back. "She's a stockbroker with Merrill Lynch, she drives a Beemer, and she's recently one of us—in the program." He was hinting that she was either out of my league or off-limits because of her new sobriety. AA wisdom suggests people don't date during their first year in the program; they are still preoccupied with unpacking and sorting through their own emotional baggage, and weaving that of another into the mix tends to result in unhealthy patterns.

I was undeterred. "Perfect!" I told John with a grin.

I told him how much the girls' mother looked like my mom did before she died. "It's spooky," I said. "And she has the same first name as my stepmother, Penny, which isn't a very common name."

Later that same afternoon, I was at home studying for the MCAT exam. My telephone rang, and caller ID revealed the number from the local Merrill Lynch office. I was surprised but pleased to answer it and hear Joan, whose telephone voice reminded me of the actress Suzanne Pleshette. Cordially, she explained that her sister had passed along my number, and she was calling to see if I'd be attending the dance on the following Saturday evening.

Her soft-spoken business tone switched from alluring to enchanting as we exchanged pleasantries. Then she explained that, due to her astute observational skills, when we met at lunch that day she had noticed I didn't wear gold chains, which apparently her father found unbecoming on men.

To this playful revelation I replied, "So am I to assume that your father would approve of me, and that having passed the paternal litmus test, I qualify as suitable dating material?"

Joan didn't skip a beat.

"Sure, I'd love to go out with you," she replied. "What did you have in mind?"

I was intrigued, though I wasn't about to admit that she'd had me at "Nice to meet you" earlier that day.

"Okay," I said. "How about lunch or coffee anytime that works for you?"

"Well, the market just closed at four, and I've got no plans," she answered. "How about now?"

I welcomed her suggestion, offering to brew a fresh pot. This garnered a prompt reply: she'd come by after a brief detour home to change clothes. Interestingly, her home was just four doors down from a house that I had rented for over a year prior to my current residence, yet our paths had never crossed.

A half hour later I spotted Joan's svelte figure as she swept past the exterior French doors of the dining room at the back of the house. She knocked gently on the side door. Before answering I paused briefly to collect myself, trying to invoke some semblance of casual charm and disguise my fluster.

As I opened the door I was greeted by her demure though perfect gleaming smile. She wore faded jeans, tennis shoes, and a knitted multicolored sweater top that accented her olive skin. Just like at lunch, something startled me back to attention just before losing myself in those deep amber eyes. I had a momentary vision of kissing her passionately while hoisting her onto the back of my white steed before galloping off toward the sunset-washed hills and my awaiting castle.

Unable to convert fantasy to reality, I settled for waving her into the parlor for the much less exciting cup of coffee. But in my mind we were off to the races.

There was a recognizable electrical tension in the air: timidity and nervousness mixed with a mutual warmth and familiarity, like a comfortable pair of moccasins waiting by the hearth on a cold winter's day. It felt as though we'd known each other for much of our lives.

As we sat next to one another on the living room sofa there was an obvious attraction, one that I'd not felt so strongly with prior new acquaintances. We interviewed each other like determined journalists, quickly extracting the details and specifics of each other's lives, amazed by the similarities and intrigued by the differences.

The atmosphere was getting increasingly charged. Finally, Joan put us both out of our shared misery with one simple request: "Can I kiss you?"

She whispered the words closely enough that I could smell the apricot shampoo scent of her hair. We kissed long, hardly breathing. There was a tingle reminiscent of my first kiss back in second grade, but impossibly and exponentially magnified.

We made plans to meet later that evening for dinner. Joan had to go to the airport to pick up her college roommate, Bonnie, who was visiting for the weekend. So I agreed to snag my friend John to make it a double date. Upon seeing John, I casually said something about being in love, but in the back of my mind there was nothing casual about the idea.

We rendezvoused around 9:15 p.m. at my house, a few blocks from our dinner destination, the Park Avenue Grill. Walking to the restaurant, Joan and I trailed behind Bonnie and John as we talked nonstop with giddy animation. It was as though we had lifetimes of details to catch up on.

With a sense of peace, I found myself telling Joan everything about the fire: my burns, the loss of Mom and Toby, and the near-death experience, which had happened on a Friday the thirteenth in August. This detail caused her to look up in surprise. Her grin was quickly followed by a jaw drop as I described how Dad called on that date each year to wish me "Happy Birthday" for coming back from the edge: August 13 was Joan's birthday. Coincidence? We then discovered that our sobriety dates were the same, just a year apart: October 1.

It all seemed to be playing out like a real-life fairy tale.

Remarkably, Joan, her mother, sister, and brother all became sober within the same six-month period. In her recovery, Joan was working with a counseling center on family dynamics and codependency issues.

We had both been cautioned about early relationships, but neither of us was willing to prevent the potential fall into love. Beyond the obvious physical affinity, another way in which we seemed to be compatible was in our mutual desire to pursue further growth in our fields of interest, and our determination to do so despite the cost or required sacrifices. We both knew that commitment and perseverance were key requisites in meeting our individual goals.

It was obvious to me that Joan was a career-oriented, intelligent, and capable professional. Diligent and gifted, she was quickly building a stable client base as one of the youngest and most accomplished stockbrokers at the local Merrill Lynch office.

For her part, Joan accepted that I was ambitious and rather concentrated in my drive toward a medical career beyond physical therapy, hopefully by becoming a physician. She appreciated the sacrifices required for me to realize my dream, including the huge time commitment of taking a full course load at Rollins while simultaneously working full-time as a PT.

In the late spring of 1988 I received less-than-ideal MCAT scores, but I still had not completed chemistry, molecular biology, and physics. I would need to take the exam again. Meanwhile, despite some interviews, I had no definite promises or prospects with regard to medical school admission.

Toward the end of spring semester, I received some encouragement in the form of a letter from Case Western Reserve University (CWRU), my first-choice school. They had placed me on their alternate list, suggesting a possible admission should one of their accepted candidates reject a position for some reason.

My anxious wait over the next few weeks turned out to be in vain. I learned in August that there were no vacancies in the incoming class. It was disappointing but not entirely surprising: CWRU is a highly reputable medical school, ranking among the top ten in research grants. It would be quite rare for a student to give up a position there.

Although this appeared to be a definite setback, I didn't see it as God closing a door. I'd have to prepare more adequately, applying again the following year, by which time I hoped to have improved my MCAT scores. It was going to be a long haul, but I was not discouraged. In my heart, I was passionately committed.

The same thing was increasingly true with regard to Joan. She appreciated that, particularly in medicine, a willingness to make sacrifices in social or family lives came with the territory. Yet despite both of our busy schedules, we somehow found time for one another and our relationship flourished.

Not long after we began dating, I took Joan to meet Dad and Penny, who were at our beloved family cottage, the "Pink Shack" in Bonita Springs. On the afternoon of our arrival, while sitting on the beach, Dad stole her away for a private moment.

In his endearingly amusing way, he took the opportunity to ask her, "Just what are your intentions with my son?"

"I'm not certain yet, sir," she told him. "But I must admit that I was engaged once to a guy and am relieved to say we agreed to break it off because I didn't feel anything close to the way I feel about your son."

Dad replied without hesitation, "I'm delighted with your answer, as it's obvious my son feels the same way about you. And I can certainly see why."

Joan laughed when she told me of their conversation the following evening. Had I been aware of the exchange at the time, I'd have been embarrassed beyond words. But it was just another example of Dad's exceedingly dry but honest sense of humor.

Deepening of faith was a central part of growth for both Joan and me. For me, sobriety cleared away some of the cobwebs that had formed through the years, clarifying that sense of certainty about God that had been fired in me during my near-death experience. Though Joan had grown up attending church and believed in God, it was in a more abstract, less personal way.

Then one day at her office she inherited responsibility for a small IRA account from another broker who had passed away. The small amount of money was already invested in a mutual fund; however, she noticed the client, named John Cross, had listed his occupation as missionary, which piqued her curiosity. She felt a strong nudge to call him and make a formal introduction. That call led to an appointment to meet him in person, despite knowing he had no additional funds to invest. En route to the appointment she had second thoughts but followed through as intended.

They met at the headquarters of New Tribes Mission, a Christian missionary organization based in Sanford, Florida. The ministry trains missionaries for excursions into the jungles of South America and other remote countries, where they teach unreached people groups about Jesus.

"You're not here to talk about my investments, are you?" John said.

"Well, I don't know. What do you do?" Joan asked.

"I teach the Bible."

"Well," Joan quipped, "I don't want you to teach me about the Bible, because I'm afraid to find out I'm going to hell!"

"I think you'll be pleasantly surprised," John answered.

They talked some more, and when Joan left she had agreed to go back a couple days later and give John two hours to tell her more about the Bible.

She returned from that appointment buzzing with excitement. John had talked about how the Bible was a library of different books, written in different styles by different people at different times, and yet it all wove together in a seamless thread, the story of God's love for his world.

"I can't explain how well this guy teaches," she told me. "It's just so phenomenal."

Joan wanted to go back to hear more—and I went with her. Over the next year, we would spend many evenings together with John as he led us through the Bible, starting with Genesis. It all began to come alive for both of us in a new way. Years later John told us that, beginning the night Joan first arrived and for many nights thereafter, while he met with us, his parents were on their knees in another room, praying for our time together.

It was an obvious blessing that Joan and I were raised in similar families that mirrored many of the same issues and dynamics. We shared a similar faith and a mutual commitment to recovery, and were far ahead of the game regarding the growth of a healthy relationship.

A s the 1989 holiday season drew near, I continued working while awaiting replies from medical schools. Having completely repeated the lengthy and arduous application process while improving my results on the second MCAT, I'd also achieved high marks for the additional coursework and aced calculus at another local college.

Receiving interview invitations from only some of the medical schools to which I'd applied, I was well aware of the intensely competitive nature of the application process. I also knew that being older than the traditional student likely handicapped my status, so my confidence and hope levels were not at their highest.

Just before the Rollins College holiday break, Joan presented me with an early Christmas present: a ski trip for two to Crested Butte, Colorado. Her aunt owned a lovely rustic home there at the base of a mountain, and it was ours to use—along with a four-wheel-drive Jeep.

About two or three days into the trip, despite all there was to enjoy, part of me was pondering a twofold question I had been wrestling with for some time now: Was I ready for marriage? The need to ask and my hesitation in answering seemed sufficient evidence that I was not. The second half of that question: If and when the answer might be yes, would it be to Joan?

As we rode up the Silver Queen chairlift one snowy and blustery afternoon, I realized a matter of surprising fact: I could not imagine life without Joan, regardless of any other goals or pursuits I may have. Within this truth lay the answer to my uncertainty.

It was a relief to settle my questions. But I also knew that should the day ever come that I proposed marriage, I did not want Joan believing that any prior reservations on my part were because I needed medical school acceptance— as though it were a prerequisite for my willingness. I did *not* need acceptance to medical school before being ready for commitment. My desire to build a life with Joan was independent of whether or not I became a doctor.

I decided that I would try to discuss these issues with her when we returned to Florida without revealing my thoughts of proposing. After all, though I knew we felt right together, I had no idea how she felt about the idea of marriage to me.

As we raced to the bottom of the mountain, our goggles shielding our eyes from the heavy flurries trying to blind us, my vision had never been clearer. The smile in my eyes reflected the grin on my face that even the biting wind failed to remove.

Over the weeks following our ski trip, Joan and I had several talks that subtly alluded to the idea that we mutually felt our relationship had the qualities we both believed were requirements for long-lasting love. In one of our conversations, I made it clear that I hoped we would continue to grow together even if I never gained acceptance to medical school. There, I'd said it.

The next day I received a letter of congratulations offering me a position among the incoming class of 1990 at the Case Western Reserve University School of Medicine—my first-choice school.

24

GENESIS

On Valentine's Day 1990, I arrived at Joan's apartment to collect her for the romantic dinner date I had planned at Palma Maria, a quaint little Italian restaurant in Winter Park. But I had more in mind.

Dressed in a charcoal gray suit and tie, I was carrying a bouquet of chocolate chip cookies because Joan did not particularly like plants or flowers—they had a shortened life span in her care, she'd point out. I also had a custom-designed diamond ring in my pocket. She answered the door looking beautiful, and any lingering hesitation I may have had about proposing evaporated.

Several days earlier I had expressed my deep love and respect for Joan in a man-to-man chat with her father and had received his approval to ask for her hand. Though I hinted where things were heading, I didn't reveal when I'd pop the question.

Handing Joan the bouquet, I dropped to one knee on the threshold. Adrenaline parched my throat, but I managed to inquire, "Joan, will you marry me?"

Although clearly surprised, she replied excitedly, "Yes!"

Both of our families were thrilled to hear the news of our engagement, which set the clock ticking: medical school in Cleveland started in six months. Fortunately, my future mother-in-law's favorite pastime was planning weddings for friends and family, so she was well up to the urgency of the task.

Dad and Penny hosted a grand rehearsal dinner on Friday the thirteenth of July at the Interlachen Country Club in Winter Park. We received many toasts and roasts, including one of the former from Dad—my best man. He quipped: "Mark's stepmother is named Penny. Joan's mother is also named Penny. And the advice you'll both get from the two of them will be worth about two cents."

There were also moments of quiet reverence and remembrance honoring my mother's role in my life.

Father Jim came from Cleveland to pray with us and help officiate the nuptials on the following day, July 14, 1990. Indeed, we were enjoying a new beginning—the genesis of another sacred chapter in the McDonough family story as it wove together with the Galbraith family. Over six hundred guests, an eighteen-member wedding party, and four ushers attended the service, which was followed by a reception at the Country Club of Orlando.

Our first dance as bride and groom was to "String of Pearls," played by a twenty-piece big band hired to provide classics by Glenn Miller, Benny Goodman, and others. Joan and I transitioned into the jitterbug and were performing a classic pretzel move when there was a loud pop, like the starter gun at a swim meet.

From the pain that flashed in my right knee I knew immediately what had happened. As we transposed our arms from overhead to behind our backs, twist-turning into our "pretzel," my right knee dislocated. I collapsed to the floor with my leg awkwardly rotated behind me.

With so many doctors in attendance, I was not short of a second or third opinion, and my diagnosis was swiftly confirmed. Borrowing a cane from a former patient in attendance, I limped to a chair along the edge of the dance floor. Ice packs were applied and the leg was elevated.

Adrenaline and endorphins circulating from the euphoric emotion of the day were enough to make the pain bearable. Joan threw her bouquet from a position at the side of my strategically positioned chair; her dear friend and maid of honor, Mary, caught it. From my static position, I removed my new bride's garter and tossed it to a gaggle of single men gathered on the dance floor.

My dear friend and groomsman, Stephen, was a professional videographer and editor. He captured the key events and added music by artists like Phil Collins and Dan Fogelberg, which I had chosen *before* the wedding. Ironically, the lyrics to "Part of the Plan" foretold the evening's (and life's) events.

Fortunately, Joan's cousin, a travel agent, was able to convert our now injury-hit honeymoon plan to explore the rain forest of Ecuador to a four-day Royal Caribbean cruise. The ship didn't leave until Monday morning, giving us an extra day and a half to visit with out-of-town guests before our departure.

And somehow I still managed to carry Joan over the honeymoon threshold, bearing our weight on my uninjured left leg.

M y first day in medical school was exciting and remarkable in many ways. Newly and joyfully married, I was fulfilling a long-held ambition. Additionally, we were returning to my hometown, where the experiences of loss, pain, and recovery had shaped the course of my life. It was also August 13—the anniversary of my life-altering encounter in the operating room.

We settled on the east side of Cleveland rather than the west side where I had grown up. Joan was able to transfer to the Merrill Lynch Cleveland office. Life was good.

Medical school was demanding, but we still found time to socialize a bit, and we both continued our involvement in the recovery community. I played on an intramural flag football team with guys from the school, and I even had time to play piano for CWRU's traditional Doc Opera shows each year with bands called New Kidneys on the Block and The Retractors.

By the third year it was time to begin clinical rotations and start thinking about a specialty of practice. *How might I best apply my unique attributes toward my desire to make a difference?* The answer came on a weekend visit to our Pink Shack in Bonita Springs, where Joan and I spent some time praying and asking God to bring clarity to my path.

As we walked along the beach that afternoon, we passed a teenage boy sitting with his feet in a hole dug in the sand. I noticed that he was wearing a long-sleeved shirt despite the heat of the day. Then I glimpsed the telltale marks of scarring from meshed skin grafts.

"Did you see that kid?" I asked Joan a little farther down the beach. "Did you notice his hands and burn scars?"

Joan said that she hadn't seen him.

"That's what I want to do," I said, realizing the truth as I spoke the words. "I want to be able to reconstruct his hands, to help that kind of patient."

We turned around and walked back to the boy. I introduced myself and told him a little of my story. His eyes went wide. He told me his name was Doug and how a gasoline explosion when he was working on a car had left him badly burned on his face, neck, and hands. He was struggling with all that he was facing. I knew then that I wanted to pursue a career in reconstructive surgery despite the residency being one of the most challenging.

That evening Joan and I had dinner with Doug and his parents. They were amazed at the divine way our paths had crossed and felt encouraged to hear how I'd overcome similar injuries at a similar age. It was gratifying to be able to offer hope to someone who was struggling just as I had. This was no coincidental encounter but a direct answer to questions I'd asked in prayer less than an hour before meeting Doug. I felt certain that God was communicating—as certain as I had been in the operating room on August 13, 1976.

Through many specialty rotations in my medical training, one experience was nearly as exciting as performing surgery. The privilege of helping expectant mothers bring new life into the world never lost its awesome allure. My rotation through obstetrics and gynecology was under the direction of Leroy Dierker, MD, whom Joan and I chose as our personal obstetrician for her first pregnancy.

As exciting as it was delivering babies for others, nothing has ever topped the feeling of bringing my own sons into the world—babies created by God, Joan, and me. I had that joy for the first time on November 18, 1993.

Specializing in high-risk obstetrics, Dr. Dierker was a caring and personable doctor. He was also an accomplished photographer known for taking candid shots of his patients with their babies and gifting them a framed black-and-white photo.

During Joan's labor he was casually capturing the highlights. As her contractions became closer together and she entered active labor, he announced, "Mark, I'm using your video camera to get this momentous event on film while you handle the delivery of your child."

I didn't have any real anxieties, as I felt freshly trained and confident about delivering the baby after a healthy and uncomplicated pregnancy. And Dr. Dierker would be nearby. As the baby crowned and looked me in the eyes, the reality of the moment hit me. I saw it was a boy and exclaimed, "We're blessed with a son, Joanie!" Then I welcomed him, saying, "Hey Connor! It's nice to meet you! I'm your dad, little buddy."

It was an overwhelming experience to bring Connor Patrick into the world. With tears in my eyes, I cut the cord and set him gently in his mother's arms.

This memorable moment was just one of several emotional highs during medical school. During my fourth year, I was doing an elective surgical clerkship in burns and trauma, which involved seeing patients in the outpatient burn clinic alongside Dr. Frat—this time as his colleague.

One night during that month, I was on call with the surgery residents, covering trauma at the same level-one trauma center where I had been brought on the night of the fire. The trauma beeper alerted us to a motor vehicle accident involving a motorcyclist. The victim had a distended abdomen full of blood and needed an exploratory laparotomy to find the source of the bleeding. We suspected a ruptured spleen or worse and were scrubbing for the emergency operation.

Stepping up to the sink with my surgical mask in place, I began to scrub. Preparing at the sink next to me was the attending surgeon that night—Dr. Frat himself. For a moment, I was almost overwhelmed by a swirl of emotions, reflecting on the many life events that brought me to this place and time, where I was operating alongside the man who had helped save my life eighteen years earlier.

It seemed that the sentiments were mutual when he said hello to me, his eyes glassy with tears behind his surgical mask.

The events driving my ambition to practice medicine and help others survive trauma were now mostly well in the past—except for one painful, ongoing reminder.

Deciding to pursue a plastic surgery residency so late during my fourth year of medical school resulted in being "matched" to a general surgery internship in Cleveland beginning in July 1994. I would need to reenter the match in 1995 and hopefully be granted one of the few and therefore more competitive plastic surgery positions.

Meanwhile, playing squash regularly with a colleague contributed to the breakdown of an old right ankle and heel scar.
While I was on spring break in Orlando, a plastic surgeon there
made an unsuccessful attempt to close the wound, necessitating a skin graft operation in Cleveland just before I was to
begin my internship.

Dr. Earle had retired, so I consulted another plastic surgeon I knew at the hospital, Dr. Anthony Smith. He recommended a "free flap" be performed. This was a major operation in which muscle and skin, still attached to its blood
supply, would be transferred from another area of the body
to a recipient blood supply at the wound site.

Called "microsurgery" because it's performed under a mi-
croscope, this rather specialized type of procedure mandated
a lengthy recovery with a long period of non-weight-bearing
status—and that was assuming there were no complications.
It meant delaying the start of my residency by a year. Once
again I had to trust God to oversee the details of my journey.

Dr. Smith was empathetic to my circumstances and knew
my long-term aspirations, and he offered me a microsurgery
fellowship studying the effects of electrical burn injuries. A
year spent conducting research and then presenting and publishing our results was a blessing in disguise. The time in the
lab would allow me to convalesce from the free flap surgery
while enhancing my microsurgical qualifications and making me more competitive for application to plastic surgery
residencies the following year.

Plastic and reconstructive surgery appealed to me in many
ways, including being the ideal field for helping and working with trauma victims. One of the most competitive and
attractive residencies was at the University of South Florida,

offering the chance to learn and train under some of the best minds in the field, including its new chairman, Dr. Thomas Krizek. The program combined general and plastic surgery training over six years.

When Match Day finally arrived in March 1995, Joan and I opened the sealed envelope together while holding baby Connor. We were ecstatic to find out I had matched at the USF program—my first choice. I felt as though I had been picked first in the NFL draft. In addition to offering unparalleled experience, the position had the benefit of being closer to Joan's family in Orlando. Things were falling into place.

25

TRUST

One night just a month into my residency in Tampa, I woke around 1:30 a.m. It was August 5, the anniversary of Mom's death, and immediately I knew something was wrong.

My right upper arm felt heavy from the shoulder down; it would not move despite my every effort. I remembered a similar experience two months earlier, but the symptoms had abated within minutes so I dismissed it. However, I'd been concerned enough to mention it to my dad.

Joan was eight months pregnant with our second baby. I didn't want to alarm her but knew I had best get to the hospital for a complete neurological workup.

I woke her gently. "I think I'm having a stroke. I can't move my arm."

We both noticed I was slurring my speech. Again, trying not to worry her, I asked her to call Dr. Rob Kearney, one of the plastic surgery attendings I'd come to know during our brief time in Tampa. I knew him to be well trained in critical care, highly competent, and someone who could help with decisions should my current condition decline.

Arriving quickly, Dr. Kearney carried me from my home to the front seat of his SUV, then into the CT scanner at Tampa General Hospital. My diagnosis was confirmed by a neurosurgery colleague whom we consulted straightaway.

I was incredulous that after all I'd been through, I was now facing some kind of a stroke—and just as I was finally beginning my training toward becoming a surgeon. My disbelief was compounded by a real fear that I could be destined for life in a wheelchair, unable to realize a career as a practicing surgeon.

This can't be, I thought. *I'm only thirty-five years old. I'm in excellent physical condition and without family history to speak of. How can this be happening?*

I was admitted to the neurosurgery service, where a repeat scan the following day revealed a small infarct of the internal capsule on the left side of my brain. Basically, I'd had a small stroke, although there was no indication as to why. I was able to walk with much assistance that day but was on bed rest pending further studies.

Despite a battery of tests and procedures over the next week, none revealed any specific cause for the hemorrhage. Clinically, as my symptoms persisted beyond five days, by definition I'd suffered a stroke. The good news was that, studies showed in events such as mine, where no cause was determined, chances of recurrence were quite low. Regardless, I couldn't believe it had happened and was quite anxious about the functional limitations I might be facing.

On my first day there, Joan's sister and brother-in-law visited and I asked them to read me the story of Job. I needed a reminder to remain faithful; I once again had to trust in God's plan.

Doctors were surprised and I was even more amazed by the rapid improvement of my condition—one day at a time. In fact, by about the sixth day, one of the chief residents heard that my function was returning and called my room to ask when I could be put back on the call schedule! Thankfully, I was able to defer until regaining all of my faculties, including fine motor function and dexterity, about three weeks later. By the end of the month I returned to work with its schedule of eighty-plus hours per week.

Time marched on. Our second son, Riley Thomas, was born on August 31, 1995. I had an excellent relationship with our obstetrician, who allowed me to perform the delivery as I had done with Connor. After all, I couldn't tell Riley I had brought Connor into the world but not him. His arrival was every bit as exciting.

Of all the people in my life who appreciated the many triumphs that followed my many challenges, no one was more joyous or filled with pride than my dear father. During the years following the fire, he was frequently moved to tears just talking about the devastating tragedy of losing his wife and son, and about the near-fatal injuries sustained in my numerous brushes with death, along with the courage and strength of *all* his sons in overcoming our family's loss. But it was *we* who were in awe of *his* heroic survival.

Even after suffering the loss of Mom and two sons, he remained a faithful patriarch. Not surprising, his personal pain and suffering quickly took him to the bottom, afflicted with alcoholism. Yet within four years of the fire, he accepted his disease, then courageously sought and found recovery. Thereafter, with God's help, he led by example, showing all of us the joy of living sober—a human doing and not just a human being.

Unfortunately, Dad's major trials in life were not concluded with the death of a second son. Around the time when Packy died, Dad was diagnosed with prostate cancer. So began a long and arduous war fraught with many battles and at least a few victories, some of which were accompanied by life-changing effects.

Initially, the best option for treatment appeared to be cryosurgery, which involved freezing the cancerous tissue as opposed to surgical removal. Of the two choices, it was less risky in terms of potential complications. After many years in remission, Dad had a recurrence of the cancer at the site of the previous cryosurgery. Scar tissue and fibrotic margins meant that surgical removal further increased the risk of grim complications such as impotence or urinary incontinence. Despite opting for radiation, he suffered the latter, necessitating bladder reconstruction using part of his colon. The procedure, called the Florida Pouch, was pioneered by one of my professors who would perform it on Dad in Tampa.

Through it all, Dad acquired a gentleness and sincere appreciation for life and its defining relationships with loved ones. As he and Penny fought his cancer from their home in Naples, Florida, he rose above the remnants of so much loss. His triumphs were further testimony to me of the benefits and good that can always come from life's toil and pain through perseverance in faith and trust.

On January 21, 1998, our third son arrived. Toby James was born one day after his namesake's birthday. I once again was allowed to perform the delivery with our obstetrician "assisting." It was another mind-blowing experience. But, as often happens, joy preceded more trials and challenges as the journey unfolded, revealing its constant series of highs and lows.

The following year, the coveted residency position I had been granted at the University of South Florida was in jeopardy. Because of faculty decline and other factors, the program lost its accreditation, requiring eight of my colleagues and me to find alternative institutions and positions to complete our training in plastic surgery.

Through another of so many "God-incidences" (the word I coined for divine coincidences)—and with the help and generosity of Dr. Kearney, who had come to my aid the night of my stroke—I found a fellowship position in the burn unit at Vanderbilt University. I had no guarantees regarding a position in plastic surgery afterwards, but we put our house on the market and Joan, our three sons, and I moved to Nashville, Tennessee.

During the following academic year, the Vanderbilt chairman of plastic surgery, Dr. Bruce Shack, granted me a position in plastic surgery at the prestigious institution. My colleagues at "Vandy" were some of the greatest I've ever had the privilege to work with, defining the years in Nashville as the best of my medical training. The diversity of trauma and burn patients, along with the quality and skill among the attending professors of surgery, provided an incomparable opportunity.

Dad and I remained close despite the miles between us, and I had some of my best talks with him by phone from

Nashville. He and Penny were able to visit us there, and during my chief year he was so proud to see me present a paper at a national meeting. The presentation was of research I'd published regarding a unique method of nipple preservation during breast reconstruction. As we left the meeting, his pride could not mask the pain he was feeling; several times I noticed him wince while standing or walking.

Several months after returning to Naples, and despite his ongoing lucidity, Penny informed me that Dad was nearing the end of his lengthy war, but he wanted to see me finish residency. As my chief year drew to its end, my colleagues and I were celebrated with a graduation dinner hosted by the chairman at his home. Afterwards, I spoke to Dad, who sounded frail at best. He admitted that sleeping through the night was more difficult, interrupted by pain. But rather than talk about himself, he congratulated me on a fine accomplishment of finishing residency.

With less than a week until the end of my residency, Joan and our boys moved ahead of me to Orlando, where she had grown up and we had decided to start my practice. Officially my last day of duty was four days away, but understanding my father's condition, the chairman released me two days early.

Leaving that afternoon, I drove through the night toward Naples. The car trip that usually took twelve-plus hours took only ten, and I was at Dad's bedside the following day. I sat there tearfully as he bravely released his grip on life. I kissed him goodbye, holding his hand and telling him to give my love to Mom and my brothers, that we'd all be together again soon. He let go three to four hours later as I listened to his last heartbeat.

At age seventy-two, on June 26, 2002, my father and best friend claimed victory over prostate cancer through death. My heart ached, but I knew he was at peace with Mom, Packy, and Toby. Later that day, Tim, Dan, Penny, and I prayed together, trying to somehow ease our mutual grief at this huge void in our lives. The next day we celebrated Dad's life with family and friends in Naples. Services in Cleveland with Father Jim followed at the end of the week.

Twelve years after we had married and bid farewell to friends, Joan and I now returned to settle in central Florida with three sons in tow. After four years of medical school and eight years of residencies in general and plastic surgery in Cleveland, Tampa, and Nashville, we couldn't think of a better place to start my practice and raise our boys. Joan's parents lived in Orlando, and we were all excited to once again live in close proximity.

With a level-one trauma hospital containing a regional burn unit (Orlando Regional Medical Center) and another multi-county hospital system (Florida Hospital), Orange County held promise for an enthusiastic plastic and reconstructive surgeon. Meanwhile, Joan could continue her work as a stockbroker and financial consultant within the partnership she'd begun in Cleveland.

Tempering the stresses of growing my practice were the many joys of raising our sons. They were each blessed with academic as well as athletic prowess. They all won first place in oration contests with Orange County Schools and competed successfully in all sports. But perhaps most telling, they each played lead roles in their school plays, revealing a persistent affinity for the fine arts, especially music. Like their dad, they were blessed with a natural ear for music and loved singing.

During my training years, I experienced quite a spectrum of ways in which plastic surgeons can make a difference: reconstruction of cleft lip and palate and cranial deformities in pediatric patients; scar revision and reconstruction on patients suffering the effects of various cancers, including breast reconstruction; aesthetic procedures in adults; and repair of hand injuries. The areas that I found most gratifying included burn injuries and restoration following trauma, along with breast reconstruction and reconstruction following massive weight loss from bariatric surgery.

Patients facing life-changing disease or injury often get hit twofold: First, they are confronted with the diagnosis itself. Then their lives are traumatically disrupted by a major reconstructive surgery or a series of procedures over time. Indeed, it has been rewarding to form personal relationships with these patients, sometimes through uniquely shared challenges as they recovered physically, mentally, and spiritually. It has always been humbling—a privilege and an honor.

One particular opportunity several years ago reinforced the full circle nature of my journey. While seeing patients in the office one afternoon, I noticed a new patient scheduled for consultation. His name was familiar: A. Scott Earle.

Yes, this was the same plastic surgeon who had performed so many surgeries on my face, neck, and hands nearly thirty years prior—only now, he was coming to see me.

Dr. Earle had restored function to my hands, providing me the dexterity to do surgery on others. Now he was coming in with a facial cancer he'd discovered since retiring in central Florida. It was an honor to help, even in the smallest way, someone who had helped me in an astronomical way. The operation was successful. A picture of us during that visit now decorates my office, reminding me of a priceless friendship.

26

SURRENDER

Growing up, our sons' gifts included all things musical, inspiring them as singer-songwriters. Connor formed a pop band called Before You Exit, ultimately incorporating the talents of brothers Riley and Toby. They've performed hundreds of times all over the United States and dozens of times on other continents, including Asia, Europe, and South America.

My practice and our lives evolved over the next decade, with many course changes dictated by unpredictable medical challenges and events. Perhaps the most tragic and shocking occurrence also affected my now-grown sons. It was a tsunami from nowhere—proving that we can never really know that we've arrived anywhere. The journey continues on God's agenda.

During the first part of 2015, Before You Exit toured Europe and the UK with Christina Grimmie, the talented and personable second-place winner on the sixth season of television's *The Voice*. They all became very close, sharing a double-decker bus while traveling with Christina's crew and her brother Marcus, who played guitar and arranged her music.

When the boys planned a US-Canadian tour in 2016, they invited Christina to join them as the show's opener. The well-received "All the Lights Tour," named for Before You Exit's latest EP, included a highly anticipated hometown show at Orlando's The Plaza Live before final stops on the West Coast in Los Angeles and San Francisco.

During their weeks traveling and performing together, Christina had been jubilant, even more than her usually excited self. Several times she expressed her delight to be touring with Connor, Riley, and Toby, to whom she had become like a sister. In Atlanta, the evening before the hometown show, she was heard to say she'd never been happier with her career.

Standing next to her on June 10 as we watched the audience of loyal Orlando fans from stage right, I noticed Christina's face seemed to be almost angelically bright. Her eyes gleamed when she smiled at me before walking to center stage to sing. Later, during the boys' set, they brought Christina back on stage for her regular duet with Riley, backed by Connor and Toby. Their cover of James Bay's "Let It Go" had never sounded better. The stage lights curiously cast a warm glow on Christina but eclipsed the boys in the shadows. As the song ended, Christina made an extra effort to hug each boy a little longer than usual in a moment of gratitude.

After the show, Christina met with my brother- and sister-in-law, Michael and Kitty, along with their granddaughter Faith; they all had backstage passes. They spoke to Christina about her music and the many fans she inspired, asking if they could pray with her. She readily agreed, and they prayed gratefully for Christina's career, that she would continue keeping God at its center. Kitty concluded her prayer with "God is good." Then she and Christina exclaimed in unison, "All the time!"

I was standing stage right along with a security guard and a close friend, Scott Buono. I was about to round up the boys and escort them to meet Joan and family friends at the side stage door when we heard five loud pops.

"I'm assuming that was just balloons bursting," said the security guard as we all moved toward the stage. He was wrong.

"We've got a shooter!" someone shouted. I quickly stepped behind the curtain to get some idea of what was happening. There were no further shots, but I could see a couple bodies on the cement floor. Blood was flowing down its gradual slope toward the stage. People were bursting out through the side doors.

As I desperately tried to call 911 on my cell phone, my physician instincts triggered an instant response, prompting me to move toward a man lying prone along the side wall midway between the rear of the room and the stage. There was blood all around him. Another body was lying closer to the back, near the merchandise tables.

As I reached the first body, praying I might be able to offer some kind of first aid, a security guard in my periphery spoke.

"That's the shooter," he said. "He's dead." Seeing the man's head in a large pool of blood, the left half of his face missing, I had no doubt that he was beyond saving.

Next, I moved urgently toward the other body at the rear of the room, a female dressed in a short black skirt and vest. As I knelt over her outstretched arms, I was stunned: it was Christina. We cared for her like one of our own, and I was smothered by a surreal sense of desperation mirroring the feeling I'd had trying to rescue Mom and Toby.

Reflexively, I asked God to help me as I focused on the ABCs of trauma care. Christina was attempting to breathe through her open mouth as I checked her carotid pulse. It was thready at best—and then undetectable. Hearing no further breath sounds, I urgently began CPR as Scott stood by, still trying to reach the 911 operators. I had to maintain an airway.

As I worked on her, I told Christina that I loved her and so did Jesus. I tried to offer words of encouragement, telling her everything would be okay while resisting a persistent doom of powerlessness.

Joined by one of the security staff, we continued two-man CPR. Christina appeared to have at least one head wound that pulsed in concert with our chest compressions but wasn't actively bleeding. I continued silently pleading for God's help—for Christina, for her brother Marcus, for her family.

As I worked, my phone was on the floor to my right. It kept vibrating every thirty seconds or so with one of my boys' names flashing in the caller ID. I found out later they had been urgently ushered out of the building and off the property as a precaution and were anxious to know if I was okay.

It felt like an eternity before EMS and police arrived. As paramedics began their assessment, I noticed police officers with assault rifles casing the room. For the first time I felt we were out of imminent danger. While concerns for my own safety had been pushed aside in my desperate attempts to help Christina, I was conscious of Scott's presence watching for other possible threats.

EMS professionals moved Christina onto a gurney and to a waiting ambulance some moments later while continuing CPR and resuscitation efforts. My attempts at returning calls to the boys failed in that moment. Scott and I continued to pray for Christina, that God would intervene. But from my surgical experience with gunshot wounds to the head, I couldn't help feeling less than hopeful.

Everyone remaining in the venue was corralled by law enforcement into a conference room at the front of the building. They began asking us about the details of the evening while they pieced together events of the preceding hours. I was able to text Joan and tell her I was safe before we were all instructed to turn off our phones.

When Marcus entered the room, I hugged him for a moment but was utterly speechless. Understandably, he was paralyzed with shock at having witnessed his sister being shot by what turned out to be an obsessive fan. Marcus had knocked the gunman's arm down, causing him to fall and likely preventing further casualties. The assailant then staggered upright while pointing another gun toward his own head, fatally pulling the trigger. I quietly prayed that God would grace Marcus with strength, courage, and protection.

A short while later one of the detectives informed all of us that Christina had not survived. Only shock kept me from screaming out loud. The numb, staring faces all around the table couldn't begin to reflect the anger, anguish, and sorrow permeating every square centimeter of the room.

It was about two hours before the detectives released us. I walked to the rear of the building where the tour bus was parked and saw the band and crew gathered in a circle, praying the Lord's Prayer.

Connor was the first to see me. He turned to me tearfully. "Dad," he said. His mouth remained open but no words came out. He threw his arms around me and we held each other tightly.

As the band and crew embraced me among them, I couldn't help thinking that here, during one of the few times they had ever witnessed me in my role as physician, I was powerless—unable to do or say anything that would offer relief.

The tears were unstoppable as my emotions pitched and swirled—such relief that no one else was injured or killed, grief beyond words that Christina had not survived.

"I'm so sorry," I said. "I tried to help her hold on every way possible, but we just found out that Christina passed away at the hospital."

"Oh no. No!" I heard someone exclaim. They groaned together, hugging me tighter with heaving sobs. My heart burned even more fiercely; I couldn't remember ever seeing my sons in so much pain. I prayed for God to somehow let me carry the burden of the devastating agony I was certain my sons would feel.

This date will remain branded in all of our hearts in the same way August 3, 1976, has scarred mine.

Into the early morning of the following day, the band, crew, and many friends and family gathered at our home to support one another. Everyone was grief-stricken, trying to hold on. Our pastor, David Swanson, spent hours loving and praying with all of us.

Two days later, community and media attention surrounding Christina's murder was deflected, but not in a way we would ever have wanted. Still reeling from the loss of someone who had become so dear to us, it was almost incomprehensible when we learned of the terrible massacre claiming forty-nine lives at The Pulse nightclub, not far from The Plaza Live.

We all felt compelled to attend the citywide memorial service the following Tuesday but were understandably anxious and edgy about security. That same week, Joan and I joined the members of Before You Exit, their crew, and friends in flying to New Jersey for the private funeral for Christina. Adam Levine from *The Voice* graciously reached out to Christina's parents and Marcus, offering to cover all expenses. Following the private event, another funeral open to fans and adoring public was attended by many.

In the wake of a horrific event such as Christina's murder, it's common to feel dumbstruck in confusion and anger, or to be left questioning our faith. Given the magnitude of our pain and the senseless loss of life, we feel spiritually bankrupt. At such times, I believe the best and only recourse is to surrender. We surrender to win, bolstering our faith that God will see us through the storms of life and ultimately cultivating light and goodness from darkness and evil. Though we live in a fallen world, he has not abandoned us.

On the surface such a response may feel cliché, a complete banality. But if we look closely we see that historically, unequivocally, without a doubt, God is with us in times of pain, trial, and tribulation. While we may not be privy to his complete plan and will, there are signs and evidence of his omnipresence and omnipotence.

Over the hours, days, and weeks following the evening of June 10, we remembered the numerous ways in which Christina had exhibited a special spiritual synchronicity with her Creator, revealing the ways God was present with her. Although she may not have had the prescience to know her fate, there were signs that she was being prepared for her journey home.

In the time leading up to June 10, God's presence was evident through Christina's obvious happiness and contentment. She was pleased with her career and grateful for the opportunity to inspire others, having recorded a well-received version of the beautiful contemporary hymn "In Christ Alone."

She also had projected an extraordinary joy and peace that night, with many speaking of the unique brilliance and warmth shining in her eyes. The way she had been bathed in glowing light during what would be her last performance of "Let It Go," and how she had gone out of her way to embrace each of the boys after the song, was different from all prior performances.

Perhaps most telling was that prayer with Kitty and Michael after the show and Christina agreeing in unison that God is good, "All the time!"

That tragic night reminds me that we never know exactly what's in store on this journey in life. That has been true repeatedly in my story. As many before me have said, we *will* fall, but how we rise again is what matters. Like a phoenix rising from the ashes, adversity can make us stronger and better with God's help.

27

PERSEVERANCE

Looking back over the many trials that inspired my journey and career, facing significant medical challenges seems to be a predominant theme. Sometimes they presented complete roadblocks; other times they were detours along the way.

Shortly after beginning my practice, I developed significant neck and left upper extremity symptoms most likely related to the cervical injury I'd sustained in the rollover car accident of 1986. Once again I feared an ominous delay, if not restriction, to the pursuit of my dream.

An orthopedic colleague confirmed my suspicions of a herniated disk; degenerative changes in the vertebrae were causing debilitating nerve compression. The symptoms included a relentless burning sensation from the neck down to the fingertips, along with intermittent weakness of my left arm and hand.

Eventually the pain and neurological symptoms became disabling enough to interfere with my ability to perform surgery. I was concerned that I was developing a chronic neck problem that might require major surgery, traditionally involving fusion of one or two vertebral levels.

A local neurosurgeon colleague referred me to a specialist in North Carolina who performed a new conservative procedure that was life-changing. Full recovery took merely two weeks.

My referring colleague validated one of my beliefs: the best doctors may not always have the solution to every patient's problem, but they will find the doctor who does. To this day, my self-prescribed physical therapy and regular massage help alleviate any residual discomfort from the disk-related injury that had threatened to derail me.

From the beginning, my practice mission statement and my personal journey have both been embodied in the story of the phoenix. My practice logo became a rose, symbolizing beauty, with a restored phoenix rising out of its petals.

Like the phoenix, my goal in reconstructive surgery has been to return my patients to as close to their original versions as possible, if not better, through the restoration of body, mind, and spirit. Having considerable experience as a patient, I always felt that without considering the dimensions of mind and spirit, efforts to rebuild the body risked being in vain. Surviving life-changing trauma or disease depends on having optimal mental and spiritual fortitude.

My growing practice had an obvious focus on trauma and burn patients. One of my most rewarding cases was with a patient who suffered burns to over half his body from an equipment failure while painting road markers on highway pavement. He underwent major flap reconstruction of his hand and forearm as well as facial scar revision entailing multiple procedures over five to six years. The facial reconstructions involved my traveling with him to New York, where he underwent facial flap advancement and reconstruction that I performed with the assistance of colleagues who specialized in the procedure. Whenever I thought that my patients could benefit from the skills or training of other surgeons, I felt obligated to find ways to make it happen.

Another successful case involved a brave young man who was severely burned in a fiery car accident. He lost his left ear, and flames destroyed the left side of his face and forehead. With painstaking patience, he underwent numerous procedures to restore the ear and the side of his face by combining his own tissue with prosthetic components. It was nearly a year before his initial discharge from the hospital as he heroically faced each day, one at a time. I have never taken for granted the privilege of having the opportunity to improve the appearance of or restore function in survivors affected by disease or trauma.

Over the past two decades, elective plastic surgery has become increasingly popular as more people recognize its role in cosmetic procedures to improve appearance and attempt to slow or reverse the aging process. This was another active part of my practice, as it was with thirty-plus other plastic surgeons in Central Florida. A vital side branch of my work centered on the prevention and treatment of melanoma and skin cancers, along with skin care and rejuvenation—particularly important for those living in areas of intense sunshine like Florida. This included developing the Phoenix

System, my own formulated line of moisturizers and products to restore damaged skin.

The long road that continues to define my own journey has revealed many twists and turns along the way; the terrain has been anything but predictable. Perseverance has been a critical factor, but one thing has remained certain: without a shred of doubt, I know that God has his hand on me.

Incredibly, there was still a further obstacle to disrupt my medical practice plans. This latest twist has been perhaps the most befuddling to date.

Several years ago, I had symptoms of chest congestion that were not responding to antibiotics. At the time I thought I had pneumonia, until I noticed some mild swelling of my feet. I finally placed myself in the care of another doctor, trying to remember not so much how to be a patient as how *not* to be a doctor. I was shocked when he handed me his stethoscope and said, "Have a listen for yourself, Mark."

The murmur was almost detectable without the stethoscope: I was experiencing congestive heart failure from a damaged mitral valve. The doctor's recommendation was to undergo immediate open-heart surgery to prevent potentially fatal cardiac arrhythmias.

Unlike with my disk problems, there were no new, minimally invasive procedures on the horizon that could repair my heart valve and return me quickly to surgical practice. I was in shock as I tried to digest the news. It seemed that yet another door was closing, keeping me from continuing my career.

Regardless of my future destination, my recovery and physical health were essential. I had to begin considering options that would improve my chances of being around for my family, hopefully for many years to come.

Whether part of God's plan or not—and I believe ultimately everything is—my personal desires, goals, and choices could not always be expected to conveniently fall in place or cooperate with God's will. Some circumstances were beyond my control as they unfolded, and I was powerless to change them—past or present. But the future was *my* choice. Once again I had to trust that God would provide the guidance and strength needed to determine the best course of action.

I was confronting a medical challenge that, if overcome, could lend itself to furthering my own insight into survival. I couldn't help thinking of the numerous occasions on which my winding path had encountered an apparently closing door—next to a partially open window I could shimmy or squeeze through with perseverance.

In due course the surgery went smoothly, with no complications. I spent only a week in the hospital after the operation, although rehabilitation has since been steadily slow. We never did find a cause for the valve failure, and while my heart function is improving, it is not yet near its pre-injury state. Occasional symptoms of dizziness or shortness of breath prevent me from returning to full-time work.

Where life will take me next remains unclear. I know that I want to help others survive major life-changing trauma and disease. I could be a consultant to those facing multiple options and medical specialties, helping them make clearer choices. There are also many political avenues and charitable organizations for whom I might continue being a resource. I currently practice as a volunteer in clinics providing care for some of the uninsured population living below the poverty line.

Meanwhile, many changes continue to unfold. My brother Dan and I are now the only surviving members of the seven McDonoughs that made up our immediate family. We lost our beloved Tim in March 2012 at age fifty-two, after complications related to a vertebral artery aneurysm he had suffered six years earlier.

Tim survived the ordeal but had some disabling visual loss from ischemia to the occipital lobe (the area of the brain that controls vision). He was also left with crippling and intractable leg pain. After extensive rehabilitation and numerous attempts at treatment interventions, he still struggled with complications and was forced to take early medical retirement from an executive position at Sherwin Williams, where he had enjoyed an exemplary career. Despite that, he drew on twenty years of sobriety to continue working with recovering alcoholics, even as he himself suffered quietly.

The day Tim died he had missed a lunch appointment with his AA sponsor. Concerned that Tim hadn't called to cancel and wasn't answering his phone, his sponsor called Dan. Dan lived relatively close to Tim's house and offered to drive by.

After seeing Tim's car in the garage and knocking on the front door to no avail, Dan had a premonition. Using a ladder from the garage, he looked through the living room to see Tim lying on the floor. Forcing his way through the front door, Dan rushed in to find our brother's recently lifeless body.

Family and friends from across the country attended his funeral followed by a burial alongside our brothers and parents. He's now at peace with Mom, Dad, Packy, and Toby.

Easing all of those losses has been the great comfort I have found in my own family. By far the greatest and most cherished blessings have been continuing to share life with Joan and raising our three sons.

Since the days they began to understand us, we've tried to share with them the joy of keeping God as a source of guidance and strength at the center of their lives. We've taught them the importance of love and forgiveness, and of kindness to others, and that their decisions will always have consequences—the best ones from making wise choices. We've emphasized honesty, accountability, and authenticity while remaining supportive of their dreams and aspirations.

Over the years, the three boys have continued to flourish, growing into loving young men with respectable ideals and values. Undergoing heart surgery has required that I put my practice on hold but has allowed me more time with Joan and the boys, who continue to persevere on their own journeys since the life-changing events of 2016. They continue to write songs for themselves as well as for other artists, performing and collaborating on various endeavors within the music industry.

One of my greatest and simplest pleasures in life has always been singing, although I lost my youthful tone and range from the scarring that followed long days on a breathing tube while in the burn unit. At one point I consulted a voice surgeon specialist in Boston, but the corrective procedure he proposed is not yet fully developed so I have not pursued it. Meanwhile, I enjoy living vicariously through my sons.

Despite their increasing success they remain humble and grateful, recognizing the source of their talents while knowing their continued success depends upon their perseverance and integrity. Joan and I couldn't be any prouder, particularly of their character and the generosity in their hearts.

Many people have asked, in light of my repeated trials and life-challenging struggles, what is my inspiration for remaining positive, for persevering in faith? What is it, they want to know, that motivates me to face the next day?

In pharmacology, a lethal dose (LD) of a medication is that dose beyond which a certain percentage of the population will die. For example, the LD 50 of a drug is the dose that would be fatal to 50 percent of the population. So, what is the lethal dose of trials and tribulations beyond which a survivor begins to lose hope, crushed in total desolation?

One may easily submit that such a "survivor" is, in fact, really just dying a slow and painful death. After all, they are certainly not living to the best of their abilities, happily gaining in strength with each new twist or turn of the journey. But when we've defined something as bad, how much is too much?

Contrary to the beliefs of many, nowhere in the Bible does it say that God won't give us more than we can handle. But much is written about how God will provide the strength we need to survive those things we fear handling. All things are possible in his world.

It's been evident to me that in the obstacle course of my life, God has been there providing me an endless source of strength to face any and all situations. Especially since my near-death experience, the signs of his intervention have been readily apparent—when I look for them, that is.

But there are plenty of times even now that I find myself asking, "Where now, God?" or "How now, God?" That is part of nurturing my relationship with him, and in due time it always leads me back to faith.

Earlier in life, it seemed adequate to apply the old adage "What doesn't kill you only makes you stronger." But how many times can we survive life's obstacles and still come away stronger, rather than being further depleted of strength and energy, discouraged if not filled with despair? I believe the answer is "Every time."

As my journey continues, people cross my path and I have the opportunity to share with them details of the challenges I've encountered, along with some of the tactics I've employed for survival. Particularly regarding the fire, my scars are telltale signs inviting questions from those I meet.

It is my belief that God allows certain experiences—some rather painful—to shape and grow us in character consistent with his desires and plans *for* us. He never promised a voyage through life free from trouble, although he's assured us that he has conquered the world and will provide the strength we need to overcome.

My scars, then, are evidence of life-defining events that bear witness to those challenges, reminding me of his presence as he sustains me through the storms. They mark the sometimes-treacherous terrain, much like the dings and scratches on my car reveal that bumps and obstacles were encountered over the history of its travels. Beyond just physical evidence, they're badges of honor that I wear confidently, realizing that I am so much more than the physical body I present to others. But I didn't always feel this way.

Following my initial discharge from the hospital I was rather self-conscious about my scars, fearing rejection from people outside of my immediate family. I frequently wore concealing clothes—long-sleeved shirts, long pants, turtlenecks and sweaters—and rarely disrobed in front of strangers. I sometimes resented myself, distraught over the self-imposed restrictions.

Interestingly, with each passing day there were more and more battles to overcome, from dressing myself to enduring additional reconstructive surgeries. As failure was not an option, my confidence grew with every victory. I began projecting a positive attitude to others. But more importantly, a positive image was reflected back to me and I embraced it.

Eventually I wore short-sleeved shirts and shorts again, and even went skinny-dipping with friends in Lake Erie! Any self-conscious fears have long been erased. My scars also remind me that God leads the way; I just need to remind myself to let him.

Since my near-death experience I know that God is with me. I may not know what the future holds, but I know who holds it. When I'm able to leave him in charge he consistently provides all of my needs to happily and gratefully survive the journey.

During my darkest hours, being blinded by pain or having to endure the discomfort of the struggle often precluded my ability to see, let alone appreciate, the preparation that was occurring for the next part of the road ahead. But I have learned that the pain has not been in vain; it's the anguish of our trials and tribulations that inscribes a deep and passionate emotional imprint. More than an emotional scar, it's a core conviction reminding me of the good that God ensures may come from "bad" things. This then comes to redefine those experiences and drive the pursuit of faith.

In my case, this has allowed me to fervently identify with anything positive that has resulted. Of course, pain could just as easily have fostered insolence and resentment. It could have bitterly prevented me from growing through the challenges or from gaining the strength, hope, and faith that I've been able to share with others who have endured similar trials. Truly, sometimes the pain *has* caused a delay in growth, reminding me that some divine strength far beyond my own is responsible for ultimately guiding me to acceptance.

Fortunately, even a speck of doubt can become incentive to seek God further. While fear and faith may not be present simultaneously, I have found that they can reside in close proximity. Even with a faith great enough to move mountains, or with an unshakable spiritual foundation that comes from a near-death experience such as mine, some anxiety about the unknown terrain ahead seems only natural.

Yet, that deep emotional imprint enables any fear to become the context in which I build the faith to overcome it. And faith is continuing to believe that God does see all the tiles in the mosaic, though we may never be certain to what extent the picture will be revealed. It means I believe the pain I experienced has been turned to, and for, the greatest good.

With God's help, I am determined to persevere, to see the glass as half full, to recognize and celebrate the good that comes from overcoming hardships in life, and to realize all of the growth that's possible—all that heaven will allow. This is my burning conviction, forged through fire.

Acknowledgments

First, and foremost, *Forged Through Fire* would never have been possible without the grace of God, without which, as they say, "there go I." He has granted me anything and everything good in life, and I remain eternally and faithfully thankful. All mistakes are mine; all glory is his.

This book would never have come to be without the encouragement and support of many people—more than I'm able to thank here. I want to extend heartfelt gratitude to my friend Bob Bourne, who introduced me to my agent and friend, DJ Snell. Both of them continue to offer guidance and prayer. Their efforts were exponentially magnified through the priceless assistance of Andy Butcher, my editor in Florida. Once I finally finished writing the original manuscript from years of notes, journal entries, and recordings, Andy partnered with me through countless edits, trimmings, and hours of therapeutic discussion. Andy's wisdom, patience, and friendship are blessings I'll cherish forever.

Of course, I'll forever remain grateful to the team at Revell, including Vicki, Patti, Mackenzie, Jennifer, Erin, and

Amy. Everyone was always a step ahead and invested themselves personally in the process. Their knowledge, patience, and encouragement were so helpful to a first-time author.

I owe a debt of gratitude to my supportive wife, Joan, and our sons, Connor, Riley, and Toby, for their loving forbearance and for their insights that have made this book even better.

In fact, perseverance through the lengthy, often painful, sometimes cathartic writing process frequently required me to tap into all available sources of love, patience, and emotional fortitude, which were granted unconditionally from all the members of my immediate and extended family, including my father, T; my stepmother, Penny; my brothers Dan and Tim; and my parents-in-law, Jim and Penny Galbraith.

Further commitment to the evolution from better to best came from my manuscript readers, including Laura McFadden, Maureen Walton, and Gayle Hemsath, along with my dear friends John and Janice Cross. Their encouragement and positivity remain cherished blessings in life.

There are too many to name them all, but sincere gratitude must be extended to the hundreds of doctors and professors who gave freely of themselves investing in my education and training.

Finally, the journey, my survival, and the inspiration to share the details of my story are the result of dedicated health-care professionals, firefighters, police officers, and first responders sacrificing themselves for others 24/7. I'm honored to acknowledge and thank those who gave me so many hours of compassion and care during medical crises at different cornerstones throughout my life, including Dr. Richard Fratianne, Dr. A. Scott Earle, Dr. Anthony Smith, Dr. Thomas Krizek, Dr. Robert Kearney, and Dr. Bruce Shack.

Mark D. McDonough, MD, is a therapist, physician, and plastic and reconstructive surgeon. A graduate of Case Western Reserve University School of Medicine and trained in general, burn, and plastic surgery at the University of South Florida and Vanderbilt University, he has served as an adjunct professor in physical therapy and worked with trauma patients at hospitals in Ohio, Tennessee, and Florida, where he later founded his own practice. Married for more than twenty-five years, he and his wife, Joan, have three grown sons—Connor, Riley, and Toby—who form the popular band Before You Exit. Dr. McDonough lives in central Florida.